THE TRIUNE GOD

The Triune God and the Person and Work of Christ

A LESSON BOOK - LEVEL TWO

*Based on and Compiled from
the Writings of*

WATCHMAN NEE
AND
WITNESS LEE

Living Stream Ministry
Anaheim, CA • www.lsm.org

First Edition, June 1990.

ISBN 978-0-87083-522-3

Published by

Living Stream Ministry
2431 W. La Palma Ave., Anaheim, CA 92801 U.S.A.
P. O. Box 2121, Anaheim, CA 92814 U.S.A.

Printed in the United States of America

08 09 10 11 12 13 / 14 13 12 11 10 9 8

TABLE OF CONTENTS

The Triune God

The Person and Work of Christ

INTRODUCTION
TO THE LESSON BOOK

Concerning the Lesson Books

This lesson book is one in a series originally designed to teach the truth to junior high and high school students during their summer school of the truth. Because the lesson books were written over a period of several years, the books may vary in style and format.

Concerning This Lesson Book

This is the second lesson book in this series. This book is based upon and compiled from the writings of Brother Watchman Nee and Brother Witness Lee and these brothers have not reviewed it.

In the previous lesson book, called *God's Full Salvation*, we saw the wonderful salvation that our God has worked out for us. We hope that you were very impressed with what a great salvation you have. We believe that anyone who really sees it cannot help but believe and receive the Lord Jesus. Praise the Lord for His full salvation!

In this lesson book you will see who this saving God is and how He carries out such a great salvation. Our God is not simply God; He is the Triune or "Three-One" God. He is one, yet He is Father, Son, and Holy Spirit. This is the greatest mystery in the universe; it has puzzled and troubled Christians for centuries.

The first twelve lessons present the Triune God as He is portrayed throughout the entire Bible. Although it is impossible to know *how* He is triune, we will see *why* He is triune. Our God is triune so that He can dispense Himself into us. This is for our enjoyment and God's eternal purpose.

The way God accomplishes His purpose is through the Person and work of Christ. The Triune God does not do anything apart from Christ. God the Father is the planner, but it is as Christ the Son that He is the accomplisher. Therefore, the last twelve lessons are about who Christ is and the work that He accomplishes.

You might wonder why we need to know who God is since we are already enjoying His salvation. These two subjects, the Triune God and the Person and work of Christ, are the most basic and crucial truths of the Bible. These truths are the "pillars" of our Christian faith. The more we know who our God is, the more we can appreciate, experience, and enjoy all that He is to us and all He does for us. With the proper and highest truth, we can have the proper and highest experience. Throughout Christian history, Satan has always attacked these points of the truth, creating many false teachings. These have caused much confusion and damage among the believers. If you are clear about the truth, you will not be cheated. Even more, you will be a great help to other seekers of God.

By the Lord's mercy, we have been blessed with a clear view from the Bible about the Triune God and Christ. Very few people have enjoyed as much truth as is contained within this small lesson book. Each lesson is full of rich points and Bible verses for you to get into. We say again that it is not only your privilege but also your responsibility as young people in the Lord's recovery to know and experience these matters. We pray that you will use this lesson book to dig into God's Word so that you may enjoy and share with others the unsearchable riches of our wonderful Triune God.

The Structure of the Lessons

The title conveys the subject of the lesson. The verses are for reading or pray-reading. The outline gives you an overview of the lesson. It is good to read the outline first to get an overview of the lesson before you proceed to the text of the lesson. The text is organized according to the outline. The writing contained inside the brackets [ ] are quotes from Brother Nee or Brother Lee's publications. The questions are intended to help you better understand and apprehend the lesson. A list of books with the author, publisher, and page number is included for all quoted materials. Finally, a list of books is included for further reference on the subject of each lesson. Nee represents Brother Watchman Nee. Lee represents Brother Witness Lee. LSM represents Living Stream Ministry. HKCBR represents Hong Kong Church Book Room.

The Versions Used in Quotes

When quoting verses, we used the American Standard Version of the Bible for the Old Testament and the Recovery Version of the Bible for the New Testament. We sometimes replaced New Testament quotations found inside the brackets [ ] with the corresponding Recovery Version verse.

The Proper Attitude Needed to Study the Word with the Help of the Lesson Book

This lesson book is not the Bible. It is a lesson book based on the Bible. It can be used as a study aid for the Bible. Do not quote the lesson book as the authoritative source for biblical truths or teachings. You must learn to reference the appropriate source—which book, which chapter, and which verse, etc. You must also learn how all the key verses relate to one another in presenting the vision of the church and the way to build up the church. Take the time to know the Word of God with certainty.

The Way to Study the Word with This Lesson Book

The Word of God embodies the essence of the Spirit. Therefore, when you come to the Word, you must use your spirit. The best way to use your spirit is to pray. You must pray before, during, and after the studying of this lesson book. It is also important that you fellowship as you are studying. It is not adequate to read by yourself without fellowshipping with others. The fellowship of the Body is necessary to help you comprehend the heavenly vision.

Suggestions on the Summer School of the Truth

It is suggested that the summer school of the truth be six weeks in length. Each week should be divided into four days, each day lasting three hours. Twenty-four days, each with three hours, will provide adequate time to pray, to cover all the lessons, and to fellowship. We recommend that all the students practice to write prophecies for each lesson, and also practice prophesying to speak for Christ and speak forth Christ. Each student should endeavor to experience individually and corporately what he has learned.

We have prayed and will continue to pray for you, that you may have an enjoyable time together during your summer school of the truth, that you will progress towards the full knowledge of the truth, and be built up in your locality. Amen!

June, 1990   Paul Hon
Pleasant Hill, California

THE TRIUNE GOD BEING A MYSTERY

Scripture Reading

Isa. 45:5; 1 Cor. 8:4; Matt. 28:19; John 1:1; 2 Cor. 3:17; Heb. 1:8-9; Rev. 1:4; 4:5; 5:6

Outline

I. God being only one
II. God being Triune—Father, Son, and Spirit
III. A mystery of mysteries

Text

I. GOD BEING ONLY ONE

First, we must be clear that there is only one God. God is one. There is no other God. Our God is the only God; both the Old and New Testaments make this abundantly clear. Isaiah 45:5 says, "I am the Lord, and there is none else, there is no God beside me." First Corinthians 8:4 says, "There is no God but one." In the whole universe there is only one true God. The God who has a good pleasure, will, eternal purpose, and economy is one. The God who chose us and predestinated us is one. The God who created the heavens, the earth, and man for His purpose is one. The God who loves man is one. The God who became incarnated to die for us so that we might be redeemed, forgiven, washed, justified, and reconciled is one. The God who resurrected to be our life to regenerate, sanctify, transform, conform, and glorify us is one. We have only one God: not two, three, or many, but one.

II. GOD BEING TRIUNE— FATHER, SON, AND SPIRIT

Although our God is one, there is something mysterious about Him. He is three-one, or "triune" (in Latin, "tri" means three and "une" means one). That is why we call Him the "Triune God." You may wonder where this term comes from, since there is no such number in human mathematics. In Matthew 28:19 the Lord Jesus says, "Baptizing them into the name of the Father and of the Son and of the Holy Spirit." Here the Lord speaks clearly of the three—the Father, Son, and Spirit. But notice that the word "name" is singular. You may even say that the name of our God is "Father, Son, and Holy Spirit." Because of Bible verses like these, we can see that our God is one-yet-three and three-yet-one.

III. A MYSTERY OF MYSTERIES

The Triune God (Father, Son, and Spirit) is a mystery—in fact a mystery of mysteries! Small and finite as human beings are, we can neither understand it thoroughly nor define it in a full way. John 1:1 says, "The Word was with God, and the Word was God." By the clause "the Word was with God," we understand that the Word and God are two, for the Word was *with* God. But "the Word was God" indicates that the Word and God are one, for the Word *was* God. Are They one or two? They are both. This is a mystery.

Second Corinthians 3:17 says that "the Lord is the Spirit." Here the Lord and the Spirit are one, for the Lord *is* the Spirit. Then the same verse speaks of "the Spirit of the Lord." This indicates that They are two. Are the Lord and the Spirit one or two? It is a mystery.

Notice that in Hebrews 1:8-9 the Son is addressed as God; then God is referred to as "His" God: "But as to the Son, Your throne, O God, is forever and ever....Therefore God, Your God, has anointed You." How can you explain this? Can you say, "O God, Your God"? This is also a mystery.

Finally, in Revelation 1:4, 4:5, and 5:6 we read that the one Spirit of God (Eph. 4:4) is called "the seven Spirits." Here is another mystery. Dear brothers and sisters, we must learn simply to accept the pure Word.

This mystery should not bother us too much, however. Many things relating to life are not understandable to men; we can only have a general idea of them. For instance, although we have life in our physical body, no one can explain this life thoroughly, for it is a mystery. Furthermore, there is a spirit within us—this is even more of a mystery. What is the life of man? And what is the spirit of man? No one can give a full explanation. If we cannot comprehend such a comparatively small mystery as man, we should not expect to be able to fully understand the great mystery of the Triune God—the Father, Son, and Spirit. There are many other unexplainable things in the universe. Electricity is one example. With our limited minds we can only understand that some things are so, but we cannot perceive why they are so. If we cannot fully understand something like electricity, how much less can we understand the Triune God!

Summary

Although we cannot understand this mystery of the Trinity of the Godhead, we can receive and enjoy this mysterious God. We cannot understand, but we can enjoy! In former days men had no knowledge of vitamins, yet they greatly enjoyed their benefit. Praise the Lord! The Triune God is not for us to understand, but to enjoy. All that He is for us to enjoy is revealed in the Scriptures. Although we cannot fully understand it, we may, according to all that is declared in the Bible, accept whatever is said and enjoy Him.

Questions

1. Quote two verses, one from the Old Testament and one from the New Testament, that tell us there is only one God.

2. What does the term "Triune" mean?

3. Can you find three verses in the New Testament that refer to all three of the Trinity?

Quoted Portions from (Lee/LSM) Publications

1. *Concerning the Triune God, the Father, the Son, and the Spirit,* pp. 5-6, 9-10, 29-31.

2. *The Revelation of the Triune God According to the Pure Word of the Bible,* pp. 2-4, 20-21.

3. *The Divine Dispensing of the Divine Trinity,* pp. 126-128, 139-140.

4. *Life-study of Genesis,* pp. 400-402.

5. *The Stream,* vol. 13, no. 4, pp.16-17.

6. *Life Messages,* vol. 2, pp. 268-269.

Lesson Two

GOD BEING TRIUNE ETERNALLY

Scripture Reading

1 Pet. 1:2; Eph. 1:17; Heb. 1:8; Acts 5:3-4; Isa. 9:6;
Heb. 1:12; 7:3; 9:14; Matt. 3:16-17; John 14:16-17;
Eph. 3:14-17; John 17:5; John 14:10-11; 1 Cor. 15:45b

Outline

I. All three—Father, Son, and Spirit—being God
II. All three being eternal
III. All three coexisting (existing at the same time) and
   not being in modes (stages)
IV. All three coinhering (living within one another) eter-
   nally and not being three separate Gods

Text

I. ALL THREE—FATHER, SON, AND SPIRIT—
BEING GOD

In Lesson One we saw that there is only one God, yet
mysteriously this God is Triune (three-one)—the Father, Son,
and Holy Spirit. But the Father is not one-third of God, the
Son another third and the Spirit the last third. No! The
Father *is* God, the Son *is* God, and the Spirit *is* God. First
Peter 1:2 says, "God the Father." Ephesians 1:17 says,
"God...the Father of glory." These verses tell us that the
Father is God. Hebrews 1:8 says, "As to the Son...O God."
John 1:1 says, "The Word was God." These verses tell us
clearly that the Son is God. Acts 5:3-4 says, "Why has Satan
filled your heart that you should lie to the Holy Spirit...? You
did not lie to men, but to God." This verse definitely tells us
that the Spirit is also God.

Therefore, the Scriptures clearly reveal to us that all
three—the Father, Son, and Spirit—are God. This does not

mean, however, that They are three Gods. We have already seen that the Scriptures tell us clearly and definitely that God is only one. Although there are three—the Father, Son, and Spirit—the three are not three Gods, but one God. This is really a mystery! It is unsearchable! But praise the Lord, we can simply receive and enjoy this mysterious One according to what the Scriptures have said!

II. ALL THREE BEING ETERNAL

All three—the Father, Son, and Holy Spirit—are eternal. Isaiah 9:6 uses the term the "everlasting Father." The literal translation of this Hebrew phrase is "Father of eternity" or "eternal Father." Hence, the Father is eternal.

The Son is also eternal. Hebrews 1:12 says of the Son, "You are the same, and Your years shall not fail." Hebrews 7:3 says that He has neither beginning of days nor end of life, meaning that He is eternal. "Eternal" is something that has no beginning or ending. This is why a circle rather than a straight line is a sign of the eternal God. It has no beginning and no ending.

The Spirit also is eternal, for Hebrews 9:14 speaks of "the eternal Spirit." Therefore, in accordance with the Bible, we declare that all Three, the Father, the Son, and the Spirit, are eternal.

III. ALL THREE COEXISTING (EXISTING AT THE SAME TIME) AND NOT BEING IN MODES (STAGES)

In Matthew 3:16-17 we see that the Father, Son, and Spirit all exist at the same time; that is, They coexist. In this wonderful picture of the divine Trinity, Jesus (the Son) went up from the water after being baptized; at the same time the Spirit descended upon Him; and also at the same time the Father spoke from the heavens concerning the Son.

Still further, notice John 14:16-17: "And I will ask the Father, and He will give you another Comforter, that He may be with you forever; even the Spirit of reality." In these two verses we have the Son praying to the Father that the Father would send the Spirit. Hence, the Father, the Son, and the Spirit are all present at the same time.

In Ephesians 3:14-17 Paul says that he will pray the Father to grant us to be strengthened through His Spirit into our inner man that Christ may make His home in our hearts. In this passage we have the Father, the Spirit, and Christ the Son. All exist at the same time. The Bible does not say that the Father existed for a certain period of time, then the Father became the Son so the Father stopped existing. Neither does it say that after a certain period of time the Son no longer existed because He became the Spirit. This is a wrong teaching, a heresy called "modalism." The people teaching this think that God exists in three successive modes or stages: first the Father, then the Son, and finally the Spirit.

We cannot accept this teaching. The Scriptures clearly tell us that all Three eternally coexist. John 1:1 says, "In the beginning was the Word, and the Word was with God, and the Word was God." The Word is the Son. He was present in eternity with God the Father, and He was God. In John 17:5 the Lord prayed concerning the glory He had shared with the Father before the world was. Both the Father and Son, then, are coeternal. That the Spirit also is eternal is clear from Hebrews 9:14, where He is called "the eternal Spirit." It was this Triune God who said in Genesis 1:26: "Let us make man in our image, after our likeness." All Three were there before man's creation.

IV. ALL THREE COINHERING
(LIVING WITHIN ONE ANOTHER) ETERNALLY
AND NOT BEING THREE SEPARATE GODS

The Father, the Son, and the Spirit not only coexist but also coinhere, which means that they live within one another. John 14 clearly says that the Son is in the Father and the Father is in the Son (vv. 10-11). To see the Son is to see the Father. When the Son speaks, it is the Father who is working. The Two are inseparable. The Bible goes on to say that the Son, after death and resurrection, became the Spirit (1 Cor.

15:45b). The Son, in whom is the Father, has become the Spirit. Thus, the Triune God can come into the sinner. The Son comes to us as the Spirit; and when the Son comes, the Father comes as well. From one side, They are three; but from the other side, They are one because They cannot be separated.

In Lesson One we have seen that the Father, Son, and Spirit are one God, not three. But, deep within, some Christians consider the Father, Son, and Spirit as three Gods. Some even clearly state this. Others may not say this in words, but they do hold this concept subconsciously. The teaching of three Gods is called "tritheism" and is a great heresy. Once a brother asked a certain Christian preacher who did not believe that the Son is the Father and that the Lord is the Spirit, "Brother, how many Gods are the Father, Son, and Spirit?" The preacher replied clearly and definitely that there were three Gods. Such a statement is absolutely heretical. The revelation of the Bible is that God is one. God is one, yet three; three, yet one. The Father, Son, and Spirit coexist and coinhere eternally. Hallelujah! We are not modalists or tritheists—we just believe the pure revelation of the Bible. Amen!

Questions

1. Give three verses that show us the Father, Son, and Spirit are all eternal.

2. What is "Modalism"? Explain with a diagram.

3. What is "Tritheism"? Explain with a diagram.

4. What is "Coinherence"?

Quoted Portions from (Lee/LSM) Publications

1. *The Revelation of the Triune God According to the Pure Word of the Bible,* pp. 7-11.

2. *The Divine Dispensing of the Divine Trinity,* pp. 119-120, 139-141.

3. *Young People's Training,* pp. 83-84.

4. *Life-study of Philippians,* pp. 335-336.

Lesson Three

THE SON BEING THE EMBODIMENT OF THE TRIUNE GOD

Scripture Reading

John 1:1; 20:28; Phil. 2:6; Isa. 9:6; John 14:9-10; Matt. 1:18, 20; John 6:46; 2 Cor. 3:17; Col. 1:19; 2:9

Outline

I. The Son being God
II. The Son being the Father
III. The Son's incarnation being of the Holy Spirit
IV. The Son coming "from-with" the Father
V. The Son being the Spirit
VI. All the fullness of the Godhead dwelling in Him

Text

So far we have seen that God is one. But this God is triune—Father, Son, and Spirit. All Three are God, eternal, coexisting, and coinhering eternally. The Father is God, the Son is God, and the Spirit is God. The Father, Son, and Spirit do not exist at different times as three different modes of one God. They are not three separate Gods, but one Triune God. What a mysterious God! But even though He is mysterious, we can experience and enjoy Him. Hallelujah! In this lesson we shall see something more of this great mystery: the Son is even the Triune God.

I. THE SON BEING GOD

John 1:1 says, "The Word was God." John 20:28 says, "Thomas answered and said to Him, My Lord and my God!" Philippians 2:6 says, "Who subsisting in the form of God." All these verses tell us that the Son, Jesus Christ, is God Himself. Some people think that He is merely the Son of God (as though He were not God Himself), but the Bible clearly reveals to us that even though He is the Son of God, He is God Himself. He is not a separate person from God. He is God. He was God in the beginning (eternity past); He was God when He lived as a man two thousand years ago; He is God today and will be God forever.

II. THE SON BEING THE FATHER

Another part of this mystery is that the Son is the Father. Let us look at Isaiah 9:6: "Unto us a son is given...and his name shall be called...everlasting Father." The Lord Jesus said in John 14:9-10, "He who has seen Me has seen the Father....I am in the Father, and the Father is in Me." Here again the Bible makes it clear to us that Jesus the Son is also the Father. The Father and the Son are one. The Son is even the Father. We do not know how the Son can also be the Father, but this is what the Bible says—we just believe it.

III. THE SON'S INCARNATION BEING OF THE HOLY SPIRIT

Matthew 1:18 says, "Mary...was found to be with child of the Holy Spirit." Verse 20 says, "For that which is begotten in her is of the Holy Spirit." Luke 1:35 says, "The Holy Spirit will come upon you...wherefore also the holy thing which is born will be called, Son of God." These verses tell us that the Son is born of the Holy Spirit. His source was the Holy Spirit. The Spirit is the essence of the Triune God (John 4:24). Therefore, in Jesus' being is the essence of the Triune God.

IV. THE SON COMING "FROM-WITH" THE FATHER

John 6:46 says, "Not that anyone has seen the Father, except Him who is from God, He has seen the Father." The word "from" in Greek is "para," which means "by the side of." The sense here is "from-with." The Lord is not only *from* God, but also *with* God. While He is from God, He is still with God (John 8:16, 29; 16:27). When you receive the Son, you also receive the Father, because the Father is with Him (1 John 2:23).

V. THE SON BEING THE SPIRIT

Furthermore, the Son is also the Spirit. Some people think that the Son is separate and different from the Spirit. They think that the Spirit "represents" the Son. But according to the Bible, the Son not only was born of the Spirit, lived according to the Spirit, worked and fought by the Spirit (Luke 4:14; Matt. 12:28), but He even *became* the Spirit Himself through crucifixion and resurrection. First Corinthians 15:45 tells us that "the last Adam became a life-giving Spirit." The "last Adam" here refers to the Son, Jesus, who died to end the Adamic race. In resurrection He became the life-giving Spirit. Second Corinthians 3:17 says "the Lord is the Spirit." It is exceedingly clear that the Son is not only the Father, but also the Spirit in resurrection.

VI. ALL THE FULLNESS OF THE GODHEAD DWELLING IN HIM

From all these points we should be very clear that the Son is the entire Triune God. He is not merely the second of the Trinity or only one-third of the Trinity. Neither is He a separate God or someone other than God. The Lord Jesus is the Mighty God, the Eternal Father; He was conceived of the Holy Spirit and He even is the Spirit; and His coming was "from-with" the Father. This is why Colossians 1:19 says, "For in Him all the fullness was pleased to dwell," and 2:9 says, "For in Him dwells all the fullness of the Godhead bodily." Christ is the embodiment of the Triune God; all the fullness of the Triune God dwells in Christ bodily. He contains all that God is and expresses God in all His riches. What a Person is the Son!

Questions

1. What verse refers to the Son as God?

2. In what verse is the Son called the Father?

3. What verse reveals the Son is the Spirit?

Quoted Portions from (Lee/LSM) Publications

1. *The All-Inclusive Spirit of Christ,* pp. 3-4.

2. *Life-study of Matthew,* p. 59.

3. *Life-study of Romans,* p. 259.

4. *The Revelation of the Triune God According to the Pure Word of the Bible,* pp. 11-15.

5. *Concerning the Triune God, the Father, the Son, and the Spirit,* pp. 17-22, 25-28.

6. *Life-study of Luke,* pp. 4-5.

7. *The Divine Dispensing of the Divine Trinity,* pp. 109-110.

8. *The Spirit and Body,* pp. 40-41.

9. *The Baptism in the Holy Spirit,* pp. 3-4.

10. *Life-study of Colossians,* pp. 151-152.

Lesson Four

THE SPIRIT BEING
THE ULTIMATE CONSUMMATION
OF THE TRIUNE GOD

Scripture Reading

John 4:24; 14:26; 15:26; 1 Cor. 12:3;
John 1:1, 14; 1 Cor. 15:45b

Outline

I. God being Spirit
II. The Spirit being sent by the Father and the Son and coming "from-with" the Father
III. The Spirit coming in the name of the Son
IV. The Spirit being the ultimate consummation (final expression) of the Triune God

Text

Now we need to see that the Spirit is also the Triune God. The Spirit is not the last third of God, nor is He just a power, or a dove; He is the Triune God Himself. When you receive the Spirit, you receive the Triune God.

I. GOD BEING SPIRIT

John 4:24 tells us that "God is Spirit." The Triune God is wholly a matter of Spirit. This refers to God's essence. For example, the essence of a wooden table is wood, so we can say that the table is wood. God's essence is Spirit, so we say God is Spirit. Never think that only one-third of God is Spirit, as some may think. The whole God, the Triune God—Father, Son, and Spirit—is Spirit.

II. THE SPIRIT BEING SENT
BY THE FATHER AND THE SON
AND COMING "FROM-WITH" THE FATHER

In John 14:26 the Lord (the Son) said, "But the Comforter, the Holy Spirit, whom the Father will send in My name." Also, in John 15:26 the Lord said, "But when the Comforter comes, whom I will send to you from the Father, the Spirit of reality who proceeds from the Father, He will testify concerning Me." First in 14:26 He says that the Father will send the Spirit; later in 15:26 He says that the Son Himself will send the Spirit. Then who sent the Spirit—the Father or the Son? We must say that the Spirit was sent by both the Father and the Son because, as we saw in the last lesson, the Father and the Son are one. The Father's sending is the Son's sending, and the Son's sending is the Father's sending. The Two are one. The Holy Spirit is sent not only by the Father but also "from-with" the Father. You should have learned from Lesson Three that the Greek word for "from" means "by the side of," and often means "from-with." When the Father sends the Spirit, He comes with the Spirit. The Spirit comes from the Father and with the Father. When the Father sends the Spirit, He comes with the Spirit. The Father is the source. The Son is in the Father and the Father is in the Son, so when the Spirit comes, the Father and Son also come. The whole Triune God comes.

III. THE SPIRIT COMING
IN THE NAME OF THE SON

In John 14:26, the Holy Spirit comes in the Son's name to be the reality of His name. What is the meaning of "in My name"? The name is the Son Himself, and the Spirit is the person, the being, of the Son. When we call on the name of the Son, we get the Spirit (1 Cor. 12:3). The Son came in the Father's name (John 5:43) because the Son and the Father are one (John 10:30). Now, the Spirit comes in the Son's name because the Spirit and the Son also are one (2 Cor. 3:17). This is the Triune God (the Father, the Son, and the Spirit) reaching us as the Spirit.

In summary, the Father sends the Spirit with Himself. Since the Spirit comes with the Father, the Father comes together with the Spirit. The Spirit also comes in the name of the Son and as the Son. When the Spirit comes, it is the Son who comes. Thus, when the Spirit comes, all Three are present.

IV. THE SPIRIT BEING
THE ULTIMATE CONSUMMATION
(FINAL EXPRESSION) OF THE TRIUNE GOD

Let us look at the following verses: John 1:1 says, "In the beginning was the Word, and the Word was with God, and the Word was God." John 1:14 says, "And the Word became flesh and tabernacled among us." Isaiah prophesied, "A son is given...and his name shall be called...everlasting Father" (Isa. 9:6). As we all know, the Word that was God became flesh and that flesh is just our Lord Jesus Christ; this Jesus is also the everlasting Father. First Corinthians 15:45 reveals that the last Adam became a life-giving Spirit. All good Bible students agree that the last Adam was Christ on the cross, ending the Adamic race. Christ, through death and in resurrection, became a life-giving Spirit. Hallelujah! What we see here is the Son who was with the Father and who is the Father becoming the Spirit. The Spirit is just the ultimate consummation, the final expression, of the Triune God. When we received the Spirit, we received the Triune God. All that the Father is, planned, and willed, plus all that the Son accomplished, obtained, and attained are now made real and available to us in this Spirit.

The name of the Spirit is "Lord Jesus," since He came in the name of the Son. So, when we call "Lord Jesus" we get the Spirit, who is the Triune God! We need to call every day, from morning to evening. When you are sad you should call. When you are happy you should call. When you do not know what to do, you should call. When you know exactly what to do, you should call even more. When you feel you are in spirit you should call. When you feel that your friends are tempting you to do things not of the Lord, you should call more, call louder. The Spirit, the Triune God, will come to save you out of your present trouble, out of yourself, and out of your situation. Hallelujah! What a way to be saved! Praise the Lord that He went through a process to become the Spirit, and that He has given us His name, "Lord Jesus!" Now we can experience the Triune God's full salvation easily, daily, and moment by moment. Hallelujah!

Questions

1. Who sent the Spirit? Give references.

2. Why is it that when we call "Lord Jesus," the Spirit comes?

3. Fellowship with your companions how the entire Triune God comes with the Spirit.

4. What does it mean when we say, "The Lord went through a process"? Give references.

Quoted Portions from (Lee/LSM) Publications

1. *The Divine Dispensing of the Divine Trinity,* p. 141.

2. *Perfecting Training,* p. 375.

3. *Concerning the Triune God, the Father, the Son, and the Spirit,* pp. 33-35.

4. *Life-study of John,* pp. 387-388, 425-426.

5. *Life-study of Matthew,* p. 536.

6. *Life-study of Galatians,* pp. 337-340.

7. *The Stream,* vol. 15, no. 1, p. 26.

Lesson Five

THE ESSENTIAL
AND ECONOMICAL TRINITY

Scripture Reading

Eph. 1:3-13; John 14:17

Outline

I. The Triune God in His essence

II. The Triune God in His economy

III. God's economy being the dispensing of His essence (life and being) into us

Text

Our God is wonderful and mysterious. We have seen that He is one, yet He is the Father, Son, and Spirit. He is one, yet three, three yet one. Although we cannot understand this great mystery, there is no question that the Bible reveals these two aspects of God, His oneness and His three-ness. This has puzzled people for nearly two thousand years. Our human mentality cannot grasp *how* our God can be triune, but in this lesson we will see *why* He is triune. God's being triune is not just an interesting fact, but it is for our experience and enjoyment! In order to see this we will use two helpful words—essence and economy.

I. THE TRIUNE GOD IN HIS ESSENCE

In His essence, God is one. That means in His life and His being He is one, always one, eternally one. The Father, Son, and Holy Spirit are never separated. They are always coinhering with one another, living within one another. They are distinctly three yet never separated into three, because in essence, life, and being, God is one. The Father sent the Son but also came within the Son. The Father is in the Son and the Son is in the Father. The Son's name is even "the Father." The Son was conceived of the Spirit, lived by the Spirit, and eventually became the life-giving Spirit. The Son never departed from the Father, and the Spirit is what the Son became. These three always coexist from eternity to eternity. They always coinhere in oneness. Their essence, life, and being are one.

II. THE TRIUNE GOD IN HIS ECONOMY

If They are essentially one, you may wonder why the Bible talks about the Father, the Son, and the Spirit. This is because God has an economy. God's economy refers to God's plan, arrangements, work, and activities. God's heart's desire is that a group of people may be filled up with Him and express Him in oneness. His way to work this out is His economy. God's economy is to work Himself as life and everything into His chosen and redeemed people so that they may be His many sons and members of the Body of Christ to express Him. This is the church. In order to carry out this tremendous purpose, the Father, the Son, and the Spirit each have a distinct function.

Ephesians 1:3-13 clearly shows us the economical Trinity. "Blessed be the *God and Father* of our Lord Jesus Christ...according as He chose us in Him before the foundation of the world...having predestinated us unto sonship through Jesus Christ to Himself, according to the good pleasure of His will...in *whom* we have redemption through His blood, the forgiveness of offenses, according to the riches of His grace...having made known to us the mystery of His will, according to His good pleasure which He purposed in Himself...in whom also we were made an inheritance, having been predestinated according to the purpose of the One who operates all things according to the counsel of His will...in whom you also, hearing the word of the truth, the gospel of your salvation, in whom also believing, you were sealed with the *Holy Spirit* of the promise."

Did you notice that all three of the Godhead are mentioned here? If you study these verses more carefully you will see something marvelous about the Triune God.

These verses tell us that it was God the Father who planned in eternity past how everything would work together to produce the church. He chose and predestinated many people to be His sons. Yet, to accomplish this required the work of the Son—"in whom we have redemption through His blood, the forgiveness of offenses." The Lord Jesus accomplished this by dying on the cross. We know that His death was all-inclusive (included everything): it crucified our sinful nature, crushed the Devil's head, and released God's divine life (just as burying a grain of wheat releases the life within it). Hallelujah for the work of the Son! Finally, we read that we "were sealed with the Holy Spirit." This simply means that what the Father planned and the Son accomplished is applied to us by the Spirit. The Father is the planner, the Son is the accomplisher, and the Spirit is the applier. This is the Triune God in His economy.

III. GOD'S ECONOMY BEING THE DISPENSING OF HIS ESSENCE (LIFE AND BEING) INTO US

Do not forget, though, that the Father, Son, and Spirit are essentially one. When the Father planned, He was coinhering with the Son and the Spirit. When the Son came to accomplish, He was conceived of the Holy Spirit. The Son was in the Father and the Father was in Him; He was even called the Father. After His death and in His resurrection, the Son became the life-giving Spirit. When the Spirit applies, He brings us both the Father and the Son. This Spirit is just the ultimate consummation of the Triune God applying to us all that the Triune God has planned and accomplished. Without this Spirit, man cannot enjoy the Father's selection or the Son's redemption. The Spirit is the application. Hallelujah! We are not a people who merely have the knowledge of God or some doctrine of the Bible. By this Spirit, we are able to *enjoy* all that the Father has planned and the Son has accomplished. Now all that God is, all that Christ is, and what Christ has accomplished, obtained, and attained is made real to us by the Spirit. That is why the Spirit is called the Spirit of reality (John 14:17).

Do you now see *why* God must be triune? He is essentially one yet economically three in order that we can enjoy Him. God's economy is to dispense His entire being into us, yet if He were only one essentially but not three economically, He could not carry out His purpose. Then on the other hand if the Father, Son, and Spirit were three Gods but not one, we could receive only the Spirit, one of the Three. We would miss all the riches of the Father and all the accomplishments of the Son. But praise Him, He is three-one! He as the Father has planned, He as the Son has accomplished, and He as the Spirit is now ready to apply the Triune God to us. When we call "Lord Jesus," the all-inclusive Spirit comes into us bringing us the whole Triune God. We get the Father, the Son, and the Spirit with all that He is and has accomplished. This Spirit is the all-inclusive package. Amen!

Questions

1. What is God's economy?

2. What are the distinct functions of the Father, Son, and Spirit?

3. What does it mean when we say the Father, Son, and Spirit are "essentially" one?

Quoted Portions from (Lee/LSM) Publications

1. *The Divine Dispensing of the Divine Trinity,* pp. 149-155, 107-108, 116-117, 128-129.

2. *Concerning the Triune God, the Father, the Son, and the Spirit,* pp. 14-15.

3. *The Economy of God,* pp. 9-15.

Lesson Six

THE COINHERENCE OF THE TRIUNE GOD
AND HIS BELIEVERS

Scripture Reading

John 17:21; Eph. 4:6; Gal. 2:20; Col. 1:27; John 14:17;
1 John 2:23; Rom. 8:9-10; Matt. 28:19; 1 Cor. 1:30;
Rom. 6:3; 1 Cor. 12:13.

Outline

I. The Triune God being in us
II. Our being in the Triune God
III. Living in this coinherence

Text

God's economy is to dispense Himself into us. Because the
Triune God is essentially one, the whole Triune God has
entered into us. Not just one-third of God has entered, but
the whole God has entered into us. At the same time that the
Triune God entered into us through our believing and calling
on His name, He also put us into Himself. So now the Triune
God is in us and we are in the Triune God. Hallelujah, we
are coinhering with the Triune God! Not only the Father, Son,
and Spirit are coinhering, but also we His believers coinhere
with the Triune God. In John 17:21 the Lord Jesus prayed,
"Even as You, Father, are in Me and I in You, that they also
may be in Us."

I. THE TRIUNE GOD BEING IN US

Ephesians 4:6 tells us that the Father is in us: "One God
and Father of all, who is over all and through all and in all."
The Son, Jesus Christ, is also in us, as revealed by Galatians
2:20: "Christ lives in me," and Colossians 1:27: "Christ in you,
the hope of glory." Before His crucifixion, the Lord Jesus
pointed out to His disciples that the Spirit would be in them:

"Even the Spirit of reality...shall be in you" (John 14:17). From these verses we can clearly see that the Father, Son, and Spirit are all in us. But how *many* are in you? Do you have three Gods in you? No. You just have one God in you. who is this One? He is the Triune God—Father, Son, and Spirit. We do not have three Gods in us; our experience tells us that we have just one in us. The Father is in the Son to be in us, and the Son who is in us is the Spirit. The Spirit in us is the Son in us, and the Father is in the Son to be in us. Therefore, as long as we have the Spirit, we have the Son and the Father too.

First John 2:23 says, "Everyone who denies the Son does not have the Father either; he who confesses the Son has the Father also." Romans 8:9-10 further reveals that the Spirit of Christ in us is Christ Himself. Therefore, when man has the Spirit, he also has the Son; and when man has the Son, he also has the Father. The Father is in the Son, and the Son is the Spirit who comes into us that we may have and enjoy such a Triune God. In words there are three, but in experience there is only one. This is really a mystery.

II. OUR BEING IN THE TRIUNE GOD

In Matthew 28:19, the Lord commanded His disciples to baptize new believers into the name of the Father and of the Son and of the Holy Spirit. So when we were baptized through believing in the Lord, not only did the Triune God come into us, but we were also put into the Triune God. The Lord prayed in John 17:21, "That they all may be one; even as You, Father, are in Me and I in You, that they also may be in Us." First John 2:24 says, "You will abide both in the Son and in the Father." These verses clearly show us that not only the Father and the Son are coinhering; even we the believers are coinhering with the Triune God.

Specifically, the Bible tells us in 1 Corinthians 1:30 that we are in Christ: "But of Him you are in Christ Jesus." Also, Romans 6:3 tells us that when we are baptized we are put into Christ Jesus. First Corinthians 12:13 says, "In one Spirit we were all baptized into one body...and were all given to drink one Spirit." First Corinthians 12:3 says, "No one can say, Lord Jesus, except in the Holy Spirit." You see, the Bible reveals to us that we are in the Father, the Son, and the Holy Spirit. We are in the Triune God. By calling on His name "Lord Jesus Christ," we receive the Triune God and we are put into the Triune God. Hallelujah! This is so wonderful. God can be in us, and we can be in God. We are coinhering with the Triune God. We are no more pitiful sinners destined to hell. Neither are we Christians going to heaven. No! We are free of God's condemnation of eternal death, but much more, we are now one with the Triune God. He lives in us and we live in Him. Praise the Lord! Hallelujah! Amen!

III. LIVING IN THIS COINHERENCE

So when you are tempted by your friends to go to some improper places like movie theaters, or to do some evil things, be reminded that you are not alone. Do you think that God would like to go to those places or do those things? If you go, you will bring Him there. Wherever you go and whatever you do, you are always coinhering with the Triune God. He will never leave you, nor can you ever leave Him. At such times, call on the Lord to activate the Triune God within you. Then walk away from such temptations. When you are with your friends, you can speak God into them by telling them about this wonderful Triune God, His full salvation, and your coinherence with Him. Then Satan cannot touch you, the world cannot influence you, the whole creation will be under you, and your friends will thank you. And God will be happy in you. Hallelujah! Praise the Lord! What a wonderful relationship we have with our God! Coinherence!

Questions

1. Quote a verse to prove that the Father, the Son, and the Spirit are all in us.

2. Were you put into the Triune God? When?

3. How can we coinhere with the Triune God?

4. Testify to your companions how the Triune God recently saved you from the temptation of the world.

Quoted Portions from (Lee/LSM) Publications

1. *Concerning the Triune God, the Father, the Son, and the Spirit,* pp. 31-32.

2. *The Divine Dispensing of the Divine Trinity,* pp. 111-112, 123-124, 133-135, 53.

3. *Truth Messages,* pp. 69-72.

4. *Life-study of John,* pp. 365-366, 403.

5. *Life-study of First Corinthians,* p. 127.

6. *Life-study of First John,* pp. 304-305, 310.

7. *Life-study of Ephesians,* pp. 410-411.

Lesson Seven

THE TRIUNE GOD AS REVEALED
IN THE OLD TESTAMENT

Scripture Reading

Gen. 1:1, 26; 11:7; Exo. 3:6; 1 Cor. 1:9; Eph. 1:3-5; Col. 2:9;
Rev. 4:5; 1 Cor. 10:4; John 19:34; 7:39; 1 Cor. 12:13

Outline

I. The Triune God in the Old Testament
II. God being triune in His relationship with man
III. The God of Abraham, the God of Isaac, and the God of
Jacob
IV. The golden lampstand symbolizing the Triune God
V. The Triune God as revealed by the cleft rock

Text

In the last six lessons we have covered the basic truth concerning the Triune God. We hope you have seen something and are experiencing Him more in your daily life. In the next six lessons we want to see how the whole Bible tells us about the Triune God. Certainly we cannot cover everything in the Bible in six lessons, but we will mention some of the crucial points.

The structure of the entire Bible is just the Triune God and His full salvation. God is triune in His dealing with man, saving of man, and dispensing of Himself into man. By this, man may become His sons and members of the Body of Christ.

I. THE TRIUNE GOD IN THE OLD TESTAMENT

You should know that the Old Testament tells about God and His chosen people before the birth of Christ. The New Testament begins with the birth of Jesus. Do not think, though, that we cannot see the Father, Son, and Spirit in the Old

Testament. In fact, the Old Testament is full of the Triune God for our experience; it is just that He is still somewhat hidden and presented in symbols. But what is often very hard to describe with words can be understood much better by seeing a picture. This is true of the Triune God. With the help of the New Testament to explain the pictures in the Old Testament, we will see how excellent and experiential our God is.

The first sentence in the Old Testament states, "In the beginning God created the heaven and the earth" (Gen. 1:1). In the Hebrew language the subject "God" is plural in number, whereas the verb "created" is singular in number. This contains the meaning that God is three-one. From the very first verse of the whole Bible, it is implied that God is triune!

II. GOD BEING TRIUNE
IN HIS RELATIONSHIP WITH MAN

Often in the Old Testament the one God refers to Himself as "Us." In Genesis 1:26 He says, "Let us make man in our image." This clearly declares that God is plural; but here, in verse 26, the Hebrew word used for the "image" of God is singular. Although God is "us," plural, the "image" of "us" is singular, one. Therefore, this also means that God is three-one.

From Genesis 1, we go to Genesis 3. After man's fall, God again uses the plural pronoun for Himself: "The Lord God said, Behold, the man is become as one of us, to know good and evil" (Gen. 3:22).

In Genesis 11, men had become so rebellious against God that they built the tower of Babel and the city of Babel. Then God said, "Let us go down" (Gen. 11:7). Again God uses the plural pronoun in referring to Himself.

Therefore, we can see clearly that when God uses the plural pronoun in speaking about Himself, it is always in His relation to man. When God created man, He used the plural pronoun for Himself. When God took care of fallen man, He used the plural pronoun again. And when God came to deal with rebellious man, He also used the plural pronoun. This means that the Triune God is for God's dealing with man. In

Genesis 1, when God was creating all the other things, He never used the plural pronoun for Himself though the word "God" is plural in number. It seems that to all the other creatures, God was just God Himself. But whenever God is related to man, He is Triune.

III. THE GOD OF ABRAHAM THE GOD OF ISAAC, AND THE GOD OF JACOB

In Exodus 3:6 the Lord said to Moses, "I am the God of thy father, the God of Abraham, the God of Isaac, and the God of Jacob." This passage reveals that God is threefold when related to His chosen people. With the God of Abraham the emphasis is on the Father; with the God of Isaac the emphasis is on the Son; with the God of Jacob the emphasis is on the Spirit. By the experiences of Abraham, Isaac, and Jacob, we can see something of the Triune God—the Father, Son, and Spirit.

First, with Abraham we see one who was called out of a godless background to participate in God's blessing and purpose. This reveals the Father's calling (1 Cor. 1:9; Eph. 1:3-5). Second, Isaac was the son promised to Abraham who was later required to be offered up to God. This reveals to us the Son who was promised to us from God and was offered back to God through death and resurrection. Last, in Jacob's experience we see the Spirit. Jacob was a person always under God's dealing. He tried so hard to make things work the way he wanted, yet God always arranged the environment to cause Jacob to trust in God rather than in himself. This represents the transforming work of the Spirit. Hallelujah for our God! He is the One who called us into His wonderful purpose. He is the One who is our promised portion. He is the One who is transforming us into His very image. He is the Father, the Son, and the Spirit—the God of Abraham, Isaac, and Jacob.

IV. THE GOLDEN LAMPSTAND SYMBOLIZING THE TRIUNE GOD

Exodus 25 describes the golden lampstand in the tabernacle.

This lampstand is a marvelous picture of the Triune God. We cannot understand this symbol in a shallow way: it is not just an object that holds some lamps to give light in the dark. With the lampstand we see three important things: the gold, the stand, and the lamps.

First, the lampstand was made of one talent of pure gold (about 100 lbs.) which was beaten into the shape of the stand. On its top it had seven lamps. The substance or essence of the lampstand, then, was gold. In the Bible, gold stands for the nature of God. Unlike iron, gold will not rust or change chemically, no matter where it is put. God's nature is constant, unchanging. The gold, then, represents God the Father as the essence and source.

Second, the golden lampstand was not just a formless lump of gold. It was gold formed and shaped into the form of a lampstand. This means that the gold was embodied into a shape; the shape is God the Son. All the fullness of the Godhead dwells in the Second of the Trinity bodily (Col. 2:9). Jesus Christ is the form of God.

Third, there is the expression of the lampstand. The lampstand is for shining, and the shining is the expression. The expression is the seven lamps. The Bible tells us that the seven lamps are the seven Spirits of God (Rev. 4:5). The lampstand, then, also symbolizes the Triune God expressed. Its substance is the Father, its form and shape is the Son, and its expression is the Spirit.

What a wonderful picture of the Triune God—the gold, the shape, and the shining. This lampstand is seen throughout the Bible until it appears finally in the last book, Revelation. In Lesson Twelve we will see how the lampstand in Revelation shows something even more wonderful about the expression of the Triune God.

V. THE TRIUNE GOD AS REVEALED BY THE CLEFT ROCK

The cleft (split) rock in Exodus 17 is a picture showing us that the Triune God is for our enjoyment. The children of Israel were journeying in the wilderness but had no water to drink. The Lord told Moses to smite (hit) the rock for water. When Moses struck the rock with his rod, water flowed out for the thirsty people to drink. First Corinthians 10:4 says, "The rock was Christ." Moses with his rod represents the authority of God's law. Moses' striking the rock shows us that when Christ died on the cross, He was judged by the authority of God's law. In the eyes of God, the Lord Jesus was put to death not by the Jews, but by the law of God. The water, of course, shows us the Spirit. Just as the water issued out of the smitten rock, the Spirit issued out of the judged Christ (John 19:34). The Israelites could not have the water without the smitten rock, and we cannot have the Spirit without the judged Christ. John 7:37-39 shows us that the Spirit would be available for anyone to drink after Christ was judged on the cross for our sins and resurrected to be the life-giving Spirit.

Praise the Lord for Christ our smitten Rock! He was judged on our behalf that we might enjoy the eternal life. That life is now in the Spirit and we were all given to drink of that Spirit (1 Cor. 12:13). Do you ever have hardships? Are you ever dissatisfied? Do you ever complain? These are signs of being "thirsty." You need to drink! No one can live without water. As Christians, we need to drink the living waters of the Spirit. Do you realize you have a Rock in your spirit? "Oh, Lord Jesus! Oh, Lord Jesus! You are my smitten Rock!" The Lord Spirit will revive us, refresh us, and make us living.

We hope you realize by this lesson that the Old Testament is not just some stories about the children of Israel. Together with the New Testament it unveils to us the infinite riches of the Triune God—and we have only covered a few points out of hundreds of pages! The pictures in the Old Testament greatly help us appreciate and enjoy the Triune God; each one is surely worth a thousand words.

Questions

1. Fellowship with your companions how Exodus 3:6 refers to the Triune God.

2. Write a short "100 word" prophesy on how the lampstand typifies the Triune God. Give references.

3. Have you taken a drink of the living water?

Quoted Portions from (Lee/LSM) Publications

1. *Concerning the Triune God, the Father, the Son, and the Spirit,* pp. 10-13.

2. *The Stream,* vol. 13, no. 3, pp. 24-25.

3. *Life-study of Genesis,* pp. 517-524.

4. *Life-study of Exodus,* pp. 471-473, 488-496, 1067-1069.

5. *Life Messages,* vol. 2, pp. 288-290.

Lesson Eight

THE TRIUNE GOD AS REVEALED
IN THE GOSPELS AND IN ACTS

Scripture Reading

Luke 15:4-32; Acts 2:21; 9:14; 22:16; 8:16; 19:5

Outline

I. The love of the Triune God toward sinners (Luke 15)
II. The Triune God in Acts
   A. Calling on the name of the Lord
   B. Baptized into the Lord

Text

From Genesis to Revelation the Triune God is revealed to us in a progressive way. Although we see a lot about the Trinity in the Old Testament, it is not enough for our understanding. It is still rather hidden and symbolic. Beginning with the Gospels of Matthew, Mark, Luke, and John, the New Testament reveals the Triune God to us in a further and clearer way. Matthew 28:19 is the first place in the Bible to mention clearly all three of the Trinity together. The Gospels are a major unveiling of the distinctions between the Father, Son, and Holy Spirit. We see that God is economically three for the accomplishment of His purpose.

Matthew, Mark, and Luke mainly tell us about the coming of Jesus the Son and His redemptive work. The Gospel of John goes much further to show us that this Jesus is the Triune God who comes to be our life essentially. John speaks more about the divine life and shows us more about the relationship between the Father, Son, and Spirit than any other book of the Bible. We have already used many verses from John to describe the Triune God and our experience of Him. There is, however, a section in Luke that we ought to consider in this lesson.

I. THE LOVE OF THE TRIUNE GOD
TOWARD SINNERS (LUKE 15)

Luke 15 unveils to us the love of the Triune God toward sinners. In this chapter are three parables that are wonderful pictures of God's salvation worked out by the divine Trinity. The three parables refer to the Three in the divine Trinity. The first parable is about the shepherd who goes out to seek one lost sheep (vv. 4-7); it refers to the Son. The second is about the woman who lights a lamp to search for one lost coin (vv. 8-10); it refers to the Holy Spirit. The third is about the loving father who receives back his prodigal (wasteful) son (vv. 11-32); it refers to the heavenly Father.

The sequence is not according to the Person of the Trinity, as in Matthew 28:19, but according to our access (entrance) into the Triune God, as in Ephesians 2:18. In the four Gospels the Son, portrayed as the good shepherd, comes first to accomplish redemption, the foundation of God's salvation. Then in the Acts the Spirit comes to find us. This results in our repentance. Then we come back to God the Father who is waiting to receive us.

The Son as the Shepherd came to the wilderness to seek the one lost sheep (v. 4). In the eyes of God the entire world is a wilderness, a wild and desolate place in which everyone is lost. The Son's way to seek us out is to die for us (John 10:15). The Holy Spirit came to find us, just like the woman looked for the lost coin in the house (v. 8). The house refers to our being. The "sweeping" work of the Spirit is to enlighten our mind, emotion, will, and conscience—our entire inner being— finely and carefully, until we are found. The lamp used by the woman signifies the word of God (Psa. 119:105, 130). The word is used by the Spirit to expose our position and condition. That is what it means to be "found." Then, having been enlightened, we repent; that is, we make a decision to return to the Father. The Father is waiting for us to return (v. 20), and eventually He brings us back into His house (v. 25), which is the church.

How wonderful is the divine love expressed in these parables! Have you ever considered yourself as a lost sheep in the wilderness? Read Luke 15 again while considering this lesson. You should appreciate how precious we are to the Triune God.

II. THE TRIUNE GOD IN ACTS

The Gospels record the ministry of the incarnated Jesus on the earth. Acts then records the work of the resurrected and ascended Christ in the heavens. This work is carried out on earth through the believers who have Christ living in them. This is possible because the Lord has become the life-giving Spirit. In the form of the Spirit He can get into them. All that the Lord Jesus accomplished is dispensed into and applied to the disciples that they may spread Christ and establish churches all over the earth. At the same time, Acts shows us two practices by which we can participate in and enjoy the Triune God: calling on the name of the Lord and baptism.

A. Calling on the Name of the Lord

Although calling on the Lord is mentioned often in the Old Testament, it is first mentioned in the New Testament in Acts 2:21 as Peter was preaching the gospel. The early Christians in Acts were known by others because they called on the Lord's name (Acts 9:14, 21). Immediately after Saul of Tarsus (who became Paul) was caught by the Lord, Ananias charged him to be baptized, calling on the name of the Lord (Acts 22:16).

Calling on His name is the way for us to enjoy all that the Triune God is, such as love and light, all He has accomplished, such as the forgiveness of sins, and all He has attained, such as His ascension. And we know that His name today is "Lord Jesus." The Triune God who was processed in the Gospels can now be richly and joyfully enjoyed by us when we exercise our spirit and call, "Lord Jesus!"

B. Baptized into the Lord

In Matthew 28:19 the Lord charged the disciples to baptize the believers into the name of the Father, of the Son, and of the Holy Spirit. But later, in Acts, they baptized the believers into the name of the Lord Jesus (Acts 8:16; 19:5). Did they make a mistake? Certainly not. Here is proof again of what we have said before: the Lord Jesus is the embodiment of the Triune God. He is the Triune God. So, to be baptized into the name of the Lord Jesus is the same as being baptized into the name of the Father, Son, and Holy Spirit. When you were baptized into the name of the Lord Jesus you were put into the Person of the Lord, the Triune God. You are no longer in yourself or in the world but in God!

Saul hated the church and persecuted the believers until he was saved by the Lord. When he was baptized, all of his past was buried and he was put into Christ. By his calling he enjoyed the washing away of his sins. By calling he received the very Person into whom he had been baptized.

You may not feel that you are as bad as Saul who threw the believers into prison. But perhaps you always seem to get into arguments with your family members. Actually, to the Lord, this is also sinful. Suppose you just had a disagreement with your mother. One hour later you are still upset and bothered. You cannot understand why she does not see things your way. The more you think about it the more your insides boil. At such a time you are fully in yourself. You "know" you are right, yet you feel miserable so you begin to call on the Lord softly. The more you call, the more the "steam" inside cools off. Soon you realize that you have dishonored your mother; you feel shameful. So you pray, "Lord, I was wrong, forgive me." You even apologize to your mother. You then feel so released and the Lord (and your mother) seem so dear to you.

This is an experience of your calling on the Lord and of your baptism. In such a situation could you, by yourself, admit you were wrong and apologize? Probably not. Your calling brought more of the Triune God as the Spirit into you. He came as light, forgiveness, and love. As you called on Him, the Lord shined on your sinfulness. But He also came as forgiveness and love. Praise the Lord! You were brought out of your self and your feelings and were put into the Triune God. We need to remember this all the time—to call upon the name of the Lord and to realize that we are no longer in the world, our self, and our sins. We have been baptized into the Lord Jesus, and we are those who call on the dear name of our Lord.

Questions

1. Explain how Luke 15 reveals the love of the Triune God toward man.

2. What do Matthew 28:19, Acts 8:6, and Acts 19:5 show us regarding the Triune God?

Quoted Portions from (Lee/LSM) Publications

1. *Concerning the Triune God, the Father, the Son, and the Spirit*, pp. 14-15.

2. *Life-study of Matthew*, pp. 829-830.

3. *Life Messages*, vol. 2, pp. 303-304.

4. *The Vision of God's Building*, pp. 200-201.

5. *Life-study of Genesis*, pp. 334-335, 344.

6. *The Stream*, vol. 13, no. 3, pp. 7-8.

7. *The Mending Ministry of John*, pp. 30-35.

THE TRIUNE GOD AS REVEALED
IN THE EPISTLES (1)

Scripture Reading

Rom. 8:9-11; 2 Cor. 13:14

Outline

I. The Triune God in His believers (Romans 8)
II. The enjoyment of the Triune God (2 Corinthians 13:14)

Text

The Epistles were letters written by apostles to various people. Fourteen were written by Paul, two by Peter, three by John, and one each by James and Jude. The main thought of the Epistles is that Christ today is the life-giving Spirit who indwells our spirit. He is our life and everything necessary for the building up of the church, His Body. The apostles experienced and enjoyed the Triune God and His full salvation. The Triune God was not a doctrine (teaching) to them. He was their life and enjoyment in all their daily situations. What they wrote simply came out of these experiences. In this lesson and the next we will see that what they wrote is not for the study of theology, but to show us how God in His marvelous and mysterious trinity dispenses Himself into His chosen people. This dispensing has a goal, a result: that we would express the Triune God.

I. THE TRIUNE GOD IN HIS BELIEVERS
(ROMANS 8)

Romans 8 tells us that the Triune God is in us. Verses 9 through 11 say "the *Spirit of God* dwells in you"; "And if *Christ* is in you"; and "*His Spirit* who indwells you." These verses tell us that the Spirit of God, Christ, and His Spirit dwell in us. The Spirit of God is just God Himself. His Spirit, of course, is the Holy Spirit. So God, Christ, and the Holy Spirit are in us. But how many would you say are in you? You can only say, one! When you pray, do you sense three in you? Of course not. You pray to only one God and you sense only One Person in you. In word, there are three, but in experience, there is only one. We do not have confusion inside of us! We have the Triune God as the Spirit dwelling in us.

II. THE ENJOYMENT OF THE TRIUNE GOD (2 CORINTHIANS 13:14)

Because God is essentially one, we only sense one in us; but God is economically three because He wants to get into us. Although we have the Triune God inside of us, He is only in a small part of our being. His desire is to fill us completely, spirit and soul and body, and He accomplishes this by His dispensing. Day after day we need to experience God's dispensing of Himself into us. This is why in 2 Corinthians 13:14 Paul says, "The grace of the Lord Jesus Christ, and the love of God, and the fellowship of the Holy Spirit be with you all." This is the way the Triune God dispenses Himself into us.

The grace of the Lord is just the Lord Himself to be enjoyed by us. When we enjoy the Lord, we have grace. The love of God is God Himself. Love is the source of grace. Grace is out of love and grace is love expressed. The fellowship of the Spirit is the Spirit Himself. When the Spirit transmits to us the grace with love, we have the fellowship. However, the grace, love, and fellowship are not three separate matters. They are three aspects of one thing, just as the Lord, God, and the Spirit are not three separate Gods. When we experience one, we experience them all. The love of God is the source, the grace of the Lord is the course, and the fellowship of the Spirit brings the grace with the love into us. This transmission is for our experience and enjoyment of the Triune God— the Father, the Son, and the Holy Spirit.

The Father is the source of our salvation, so Paul said, "the love of God." Christ the Son's coming is for the accomplishment of salvation and our full enjoyment of God, so he said, "the grace of the Lord." The Spirit whom Christ became is the transmission into us of all that the Father is and all that Christ has accomplished; thus Paul called this "the fellowship of the Holy Spirit." The whole Triune God is working in oneness to dispense His Being into us. Eventually, our spirit and soul and body will be saturated with Him. Hallelujah!

Second Corinthians 13:14, then, is strong proof that God is triune for our experience, not just for teaching. Paul did not just say, "The Father, Son, and Holy Spirit be with you all." Yes, he mentioned the Trinity, but as grace, love, and fellowship. This is very experiential and shows God's dispensing. But how do we experience and enjoy His dispensing? And what should be the result? In the church, everyone is encouraged to read God's Word, pray, and call on His name. That is absolutely right; but you should always remember that God's dispensing is for producing His expression. Our reading, praying, and calling should affect our lives at home and at school. Our enjoyment is not just for ourselves; it is for God to be lived out of us.

What does it mean for God to be lived out and expressed through us? Consider righteousness, for example. God is righteous. He is absolutely right and honest in everything He does. What about us? In ourselves we are not righteous. Suppose you bought something at the store and by mistake the checker did not charge you enough money. Most young people today would never say anything. In fact, they would be so happy to have saved some money. But that is unrighteous. That is the expression of the Devil. You might say that it was the store's fault or that they charge too much anyway. Those excuses just show how much you love your money and how unrighteous you are. Actually, to keep that money is the same as stealing.

Suppose at that time you prayed: "Lord, I know I should say something, but I can't. Lord Jesus, I am not righteous but You are—I just turn to You." After praying like that do you think you could keep the extra money? No, you would pay the proper amount. That is the Triune God lived out of you as righteousness. In yourself you would just walk out of the store happily, but by turning to the Lord you allow Him to dispense Himself into you so you could pay the money. You take in more of the righteous God. The people in the world express unrighteousness, but because of experiencing God's dispensing you express God as righteousness.

God's goal is a group of people that are full of Him so they can express Him. The church should have the highest expression in the universe. We should express everything that God is. God is love; He loves even His enemies. God is forgiving; He forgives the worst sin. But we cannot even love our own brother or sister, nor can we forgive the smallest sin. So day by day we need to experience and enjoy the Triune God. We need to pray, call on His name, and read the Word so that He could dispense more of Himself into us so that we could express Him.

He is so wonderful. He is so experiential. He is so enjoyable. His goal is to make us His sons that we may be members of the Body of Christ to express Him. He can reach His goal through this type of enjoyment. It is so easy. Hallelujah for the dispensing of our Triune God! Praise the Lord for the goal of God's full salvation!

Questions

1. Use 2 Corinthians 13:14 to write a prophesy concerning the enjoyment of the Triune God.

Quoted Portions from (Lee/LSM) Publications

1. *Life Messages,* vol. 2, pp. 164-166.

2. *Life-study of Romans,* pp. 628-630.

3. *Life-study of Second Corinthians,* pp. 523-526.

4. *The Divine Dispensing of the Divine Trinity,* pp. 399-401, 403-405.

Lesson Ten

THE TRIUNE GOD AS REVEALED
IN THE EPISTLES (2)

Scripture Reading

Eph. 2:1-6, 13, 17-18; 1 Cor. 15:45b; Eph. 3:14-17

Outline

III. The two-way traffic of the Triune God (Ephesians 2)

IV. The indwelling of the Triune God (Ephesians 3)

Text

In this lesson we will look at Ephesians chapters two and three. Ephesians 2 shows us a wonderful two-way traffic. It shows God coming to us, then us going back to God.

III. THE TWO-WAY TRAFFIC OF
THE TRIUNE GOD
(EPHESIANS 2)

Ephesians 2 starts by showing that we were fallen into sin and death and that we were even walking in the realm of sin and death (vv. 1-3). But God, because of His great love, came to enliven us, to raise us up from the dead, and to exalt us and seat us in the heavens. But He did not do this directly—He did it through Christ. Without Christ there is no way for God to enliven us. He raised us up and seated us in the heavens in Christ (vv. 4-6). Christ is the means, the element, and the sphere for God to enliven us, to raise us up, and to seat us in the heavens. Outside of Christ God has no way to work out these three matters. God did it, but He did it through a channel, through Christ.

As God's channel, Christ did many things. All He did can be summed up in the matter of His blood (v. 13). The blood is the sign of Christ's marvelous death. After Christ accomplished so much by His all-inclusive death, He came to preach the gospel (v. 17). How could He preach the gospel to us after

He was crucified and buried? The answer is that He resurrected to become the life-giving Spirit (1 Cor. 15:45b). When Christ as the Spirit preached such a gospel, we heard and accepted it. What then did we receive? We received the life-giving Spirit. Hallelujah! What started with God's love has come through Christ, the channel, and has reached us as the Spirit!

This, however, is not the goal. The Triune God ultimately wants to bring us into Himself. So, 2:18 continues, "For through Him we both have access in one Spirit unto the Father." These verses show us that when we receive the Son in His preaching, we receive the Spirit. The Spirit then brings us back to the Father through the Son. This is marvelous! The Father came to us through the Son in the Spirit, and now the Spirit brings us back to the Father, through the Son. What a wonderful two-way traffic! We enjoy the threefold dispensing of life by the Triune God.

IV. THE INDWELLING OF THE TRIUNE GOD (EPHESIANS 3)

Following Ephesians 2, chapter 3 has a prayer by the Apostle Paul. Ephesians 3:14-17 says, "I bow my knees unto the *Father*...that He would grant you...to be strengthened with power through *His Spirit* into the inner man, that *Christ* may make His home in your hearts through faith." Here we see again the Triune God—the Father, His Spirit, and Christ. This is a wonderful prayer for our experience of the divine dispensing of the divine Trinity. First, Paul bowed His knees to the Father. This means that he appealed to the source. He asked that the Father strengthen the believers through His Spirit into the inner man. Our inner man is our spirit that has been regenerated by the Holy Spirit. Our spirit is mingled with the Spirit. How can we be one spirit with the Lord? It is only by the Lord as the Spirit mingling Himself with our spirit. The divine Spirit has mingled with our human spirit to become one spirit. This is wonderful. The Father strengthens us through the Spirit into our inner man.

What does it mean to be strengthened with power through the Spirit into our inner man? Let us consider our experience. Many times we Christians become bothered, puzzled, or even disappointed. Nothing seems to go right in school or at home. The more we look at our situation, the more we feel that we are stuck and do not know what to do. The more we think this way, the more we are weakened and deceived. At that time we need to say, "Satan, get away from me! I will enter into my inner man. I will enjoy the strengthening of the Spirit in my spirit." If you go on to pray a few more minutes, you will be strengthened even more. By praying, you exercise your spirit that is mingled with His Spirit. This strengthens you into your inner man. You need to practice this to enjoy the Triune God.

Paul goes on to say that when we are strengthened this way, Christ the Son may make His home in our hearts. This means that Christ settles down in our whole being. Our heart is made up of our soul (mind, emotion, and will) plus our conscience. (Our conscience is part of our spirit.) We are Christians already, and Christ is in us; yet He wants to make His home in our entire heart. He does not want to be in just one part, but He wants to live in every part of us. Too many times we do not feel that we are strong in our spirit. The reason for this is that we have Christ in only a small part of us. If He occupied every "room" of our heart we could never be weak.

When you first received the Lord, He came into your spirit. This is like letting Him into your "living room." But you may not have given Him the freedom to move into another part. Your mind, for example, is another "room" that Christ would like to move into. Sometimes you think about things that you should not. You may sense that the Lord wants you to stop such thinking and to begin calling on His name. But when you do not, you miss an opportunity to let Him make His home in more of your heart. What about your emotions? You may like a certain thing or person more than the Lord. The Lord wants you to love Him with all of your heart, but you do not turn back to Him. Then how about your will? The Lord wants you to read the Word but you refuse.

Throughout your daily life there are many opportunities for the Lord to move into more rooms of your heart. At such times, you need to be softened in your heart and you need to repent to the Lord. Then you will enjoy the Spirit's strengthening and the Lord's salvation of your whole being, till your mind, emotion, will, and conscience are filled with Christ. This is how Christ can make His home in your heart.

Although in Lessons Nine and Ten we covered only a few portions from some of the Epistles, we can appreciate how rich they are in showing us how to experience the Triune God. By pointing out some of the verses concerning the Triune God, we believe you will be helped to see some of the same kinds of things on your own. With such help we hope you will want to read more of the Epistles to enjoy and experience the dispensing of our wonderful God.

Questions

1. What is the "two-way traffic" referred to in this lesson?

2. Are you allowing the Spirit to occupy more and more of your being? Give some examples.

3. Memorize Ephesians 3:14-17.

Quoted Portions from (Lee/LSM) Publications

1. *The Divine Dispensing of the Divine Trinity,* pp. 157-164, 170-175.

2. *Life-study of Ephesians,* p. 297.

THE TRIUNE GOD AS REVEALED IN REVELATION

Scripture Reading

Rev. 1:1, 4-5, 7; 21:12-13; 22:1; John 7:37-39; Eph. 3:9; John 1:29; Eph. 1:7; John 3:6

Outline

I. Grace and peace from the Triune God
II. The speaking Spirit
III. The Triune God shown by the New Jerusalem
    A. The Triune God as our entrance
    B. The Triune God as our existence

Text

In this lesson we come to the last book of the Bible, Revelation. The whole Bible is the unveiling of God, and Revelation is the conclusion of the entire Bible. So in this book we have the ultimate and complete revelation of who God is. God is triune. In Revelation, the book which reveals things in an ultimate way, we see something deeper, higher, richer, and sweeter concerning the Triune God.

I. GRACE AND PEACE FROM THE TRIUNE GOD

In chapter one there is a wonderful greeting. Revelation 1:4 and 5 say, "Grace to you and peace from Him who is, and who was, and who is coming, and from the seven Spirits who are before His throne, and from Jesus Christ, the faithful Witness, the Firstborn of the dead, and the Ruler of the kings of the earth." Here it says that you will receive grace and peace from the Triune God. He "who is, and who was, and who is coming" is God the eternal Father. The "seven Spirits who are before His throne" are God the Spirit. Jesus Christ, of course, is God the Son. He is the faithful Witness, the

Firstborn of the dead, and the Ruler of the kings of the earth. Most of the Epistles begin with a greeting but none can compare with this one. This is the ultimate "Triune God greeting." If you would pray-read this verse, you could not help but enjoy grace and peace from the Triune God.

II. THE SPEAKING SPIRIT

In chapters two and three we see that the Lord is just the Spirit. In these chapters there are seven epistles to seven local churches. At the beginning of each epistle it is the Lord who speaks (2:1, 8, 12, 18; 3:1, 7, 14). But at the end of all seven epistles it says that it is the Spirit speaking (2:7, 11, 17, 29; 3:6, 13, 22). This proves that whenever the Lord Jesus speaks He is the speaking Spirit. The Lord is the Spirit and the Spirit is the Lord. The speaking Lord is the speaking Spirit.

Have you ever heard the Lord's speaking? Certainly you cannot hear Him with your physical ears. But because Christ is the speaking Spirit, He can speak something into your spirit, your "spiritual ears." When you read the Word of God with an open spirit, the Spirit will speak something of Christ into you. In the letter to Ephesus the Lord says, "But I have this against you, that you have left your first love. Remember therefore whence you have fallen and repent" (Rev. 2:4-5). Then verse 7 says, "He who has an ear, let him hear what the Spirit says to the churches." As you read these verses you may realize that the Lord is not your first love, your best love. That means you love something else—like clothing, music, or computer games—more than the Lord Himself. That feeling inside you is from the speaking Spirit. That is the Lord speaking to you. You must immediately repent and turn back to Him by praying, "O Lord, I love You only. I don't care for so many other things. I want to be crazily in love with You. I love You supremely. You are my best love, my first love." Then the grace and peace of the Triune God will fill you. You will enjoy the presence of the Lord as grace and your heart will be at peace with God. Hallelujah, He loves us so much! He should be our first love.

III. THE TRIUNE GOD
SHOWN BY THE NEW JERUSALEM

The New Jerusalem in chapters twenty-one and twenty-two unveils the Triune God to us in an ultimate way. All the features of the holy city that John describes are wonderful signs showing us the Triune God and His economy. We shall look at just two of those features.

A. The Triune God as Our Entrance

Revelation 21:12 and 13 tell us that this city has "a great and high wall; having twelve gates...on the east three gates, and on the north three gates, and on the south three gates, and on the west three gates." The three gates on each side signify that the Triune God—the Father, Son, and Spirit—works together to bring people into the holy city. This is indicated by the three parables in Luke 15. We saw in Lesson Eight that in order for a sinner to be brought to the Father's house, there is the need of the Son, the Shepherd, to bring back the lost sheep; there is the need of the Spirit to enlighten people's hearts that they may repent; and there is the need of the Father to receive the returned and repentant prodigal son. Hence the Triune God is the entrance to the New Jerusalem.

Each of the four sides of the city has three gates. The gates on any one side are exactly the same as the gates on the other three sides. This indicates that the Triune God is available to people in all four corners of the earth. Whether you come from the east, north, south or west, there is an entrance into the holy city. (We will see in the next lesson that the New Jerusalem is not a physical city but rather the Triune God mingled with His people.) What an entrance this city has!

B. The Triune God as Our Existence

Verse 1 of chapter twenty-two says, "And he showed me a river of water of life, bright as crystal, proceeding out of the throne of God and of the Lamb." Here we see the Triune God in full. There is God, the Lamb, and the river, which represents the Spirit (John 7:38-39). Notice that there are not two thrones—one for God and one for the Lamb. There is only one throne. Then how do They sit? Are They side by side or are They one on top of another? By now you should know that God is in the Lamb and the Lamb is in God. They coinhere one another. And out of this throne, God the Spirit is flowing out as a river. When the Spirit reaches you, you have both the Father and the Son.

This scene shows us the Triune God for our existence. First, God the Father is the Creator (Eph. 3:9). He created all things, including you and me. If He did not create us, we would not exist. So we must thank Him for being the creating God. Second, the Son as the Lamb is our Redeemer (John 1:29; Eph. 1:7). He shed His blood for our sins that we might be redeemed back to God. Without His redemption we would be under God's condemnation forever—in the lake of fire. So we must praise Him, our redeeming Lamb! Finally, the Spirit, shown by the river of life, is our Regenerator (John 3:6). The Spirit regenerated us so that we are born of God. Then He continually supplies us so that we may grow in God and express Him. That is for our existence as children of God. We should greatly appreciate such a three-one God for our three-fold existence; He is our Creator, Redeemer, and Regenerator.

Questions

1. Pray-read Revelation 22:1-2 with your companions.

2. Explain how Revelation 22:1-2 reveals the Triune God.

Quoted Portions from (Lee/LSM) Publications

1. *Life-study of Revelation,* pp. 37-45, 121-124, 720-722, 740-744.

2. *Life-study of Hebrews,* p. 29.

3. *The Basic Revelation in the Holy Scriptures,* p. 133.

4. *The Vision of God's Building,* pp. 200-201.

Lesson Twelve

THE CONSUMMATION OF THE DISPENSING OF THE TRIUNE GOD

Scripture Reading

Rev. 1:20; John 15:1, 5, 16; Rev. 1:1;
21:2-3, 9, 22; 4:3; 2 Pet. 1:4; Rev. 21:18

Outline

I. Seven golden lampstands
II. The vine and the branches
   A. The Triune God
   B. The believers
   C. Bearing fruit
III. The New Jerusalem
   A. A mutual habitation
   B. Possessing God's life and nature
IV. Our eternal destination

Text

We have seen many wonderful and mysterious things about the Triune God. Although we cannot understand how our God can be three-one, we have seen that He is three-one in order to dispense Himself into us. In this last lesson on the Triune God we want to see the final result, the consummation, of His dispensing. Such a rich Triune God is doing so much for us. He is dispensing Himself into us as life and everything. But there must be an issue; something must be produced by His economy.

I. SEVEN GOLDEN LAMPSTANDS

In Lesson Seven we saw how the golden lampstand in Exodus 25 is a wonderful type of the Triune God. That lampstand also appears in 1 Kings 7, then in Zechariah 4. Each time it reveals more to us about the Triune God, and each time it is related to God's dwelling place. But the final appearance shows us the goal. In Revelation 1:12 John saw a vision of seven golden lampstands. This was a great mystery to him, so the Lord told him that "the seven lampstands are seven churches" (1:20). The lampstand that symbolized the Triune God has now become the seven lampstands which are the seven churches!

But the church is made up of people. How could the lampstand be a symbol of both the Triune God and the church? This is possible because the church is just the mingling of God and man. By working Himself into man, God has produced the churches as the golden lampstands. They are filled with the divine nature of God. Christ has made His home in the believers' hearts; the Spirit has saturated their whole being, so they have become the full expression of the Triune God. They are golden and they are shining. When people see the church they see the Triune God.

II. THE VINE AND THE BRANCHES

In John 15 the Lord Jesus describes God's economy as a vine tree. In 15:1 Jesus says: "I am the true vine, and My Father is the husbandman." In 15:5 He says, "I am the vine, you are the branches; he who abides in Me and I in him, he bears much fruit."

A. The Triune God

The vine tree is a picture of the Triune God. The Father is the husbandman (farmer). He is the source and originator of this vine tree. It was planted by Him and is cultivated and supplied by Him. He is even its soil, its sunshine, and its air. The Lord said, "I am the vine." The Son is the vine, which is the embodiment of the Father. All that the Father is, has, and does is wrapped up in this vine. Later, in John 15:26, the Spirit is revealed as the Spirit of reality. We know this Spirit brings all that the Father is and has, and makes it our reality. The Spirit is the sap, the life juice, that flows in the vine.

This great vine is the organism of the Triune God. An organism is something that is living. All that the Father is is in this organism, embodied in this vine, which is the Second of the Trinity. Within the vine is the circulating life-flow of the Spirit. It is the Spirit who carries the riches of the Father to sustain the vine and its branches.

B. The Believers

But in this picture there is not only the Triune God; we are also a part of this wonderful vine tree. The Lord says, "I am the vine, you are the branches." The branches of the vine are its body; if you cut off all the branches you would be left with just a bare stem. There would be no body and no branching out. In the same way, the church is the Body of Christ. We are the branches of the vine. We live in the vine and the Spirit flows through us, bringing us all the riches of the Triune God. In this way we are the expression of the Triune God, the branching out of God. We are vital to Him, for without us He has no way to be fully expressed.

The picture in John 15 shows us what the Body of Christ is. It is the Triune God and His believers blended into one living organism. The church is not an organization; it is an organism. The ultimate intention of the Triune God is that He might be worked into us and mingled with us until He and we become a mutual abode. That means God abides in us and we abide in Him. Wonderful!

C. Bearing Fruit

By this abiding, the branches of the vine bear fruit. As we receive the dispensing of the Triune God into us, we should dispense Him into others to bear them as fruit. This is our responsibility and joy (John 15:8, 11, 16). A vine tree is only good for bearing fruit, and a rich vine should bear much fruit. No husbandman wants a vine that does not bear fruit. The abundant fruit is the husbandman's glory. Bearing fruit is our occupation and the Father's glory.

We enjoy God in such a rich way. Don't you think that it is right for us to tell our friends so that they may also enjoy this God? If we do not tell our friends about this wonderful Triune God, how can they believe and receive Him? When we speak, we branch out God. Since we are His branches, we can branch Him out to reach our friends. What a privilege! We are not only the receivers of God, but we are also the dispensers of God. We work together with God to bring others into the vine, into the organism of the Triune God. Hallelujah! Then the Father will get the glory through us.

III. THE NEW JERUSALEM

The New Jerusalem is the ultimate consummation of the dispensing of the Triune God into His chosen and redeemed people. Many people think that the New Jerusalem is a physical city or is "heaven." But according to Revelation 1:1, all the things revealed in Revelation are signs and symbols. In Ephesians 5, the church is the bride of Christ. Revelation 21:2 and 9 say that the New Jerusalem is the bride. So the New Jerusalem is not a physical place or the so-called "heaven"; rather, it is the enlargement, completion, fullness, and ultimate expression of the church. It is the mingling of the Triune God and humanity.

A. A Mutual Habitation

Revelation 21:3 tells us that the New Jerusalem is the tabernacle of God. This means that it is God's dwelling place. However, 21:22 shows us that the holy city is the temple of His people. What does this mean? This means that God lives in His people and His people live in Him. The New Jerusalem is the mutual habitation of God and man. After many generations of dispensing Himself into His people, God and His people coinhere one another. Hallelujah! Would you like to go to heaven or would you rather be in this coinherence? "Going to heaven to be with God" is too poor compared to such a coinherence. To live in the Triune God and to have the Triune God live in us is the greatest blessing in the universe.

B. Possessing God's Life and Nature

Revelation 21:18 says that "the building material of its wall was jasper; and the city was pure gold." Verse 11 says that the light of the New Jerusalem "was like a most precious stone, as a jasper stone, clear as crystal." Jasper is dark green. It signifies life in its richness. Green grass, green fields, and green mountains all testify of the richness of life. If a field is brown we have the impression that there is no life there. The great wall of the New Jerusalem is a shining testimony of the richness of God's life. Revelation 4:3 says that God Himself has the appearance of jasper stone. Keep in mind that the New Jerusalem is just the enlargement of the church. That means that one day God's people will have the appearance of God. Praise the Lord! We will fully express the richness of God's life!

Within the wall, the city is of pure gold. You will recall that gold symbolizes God's divine nature. This means that we, God's people, will be fully constituted with God's nature. Outwardly the city is green, expressing the divine life; inwardly it is gold, full of the divine nature. This is truly a glorious picture! This is the ultimate result of the dispensing of the Triune God. The more He dispenses Himself into us, the more we receive His divine nature. Once we were going to the lake of fire, now we are going into God. Originally, we were full of the satanic nature; at the end, we will be full of the divine nature. The only way to get from here to there is to receive more of His dispensing. We need to escape the corruption that is in the world in order to partake of the divine nature (2 Pet. 1:4). O Lord Jesus! What a way! What a conclusion!

IV. OUR ETERNAL DESTINATION

God's eternal desire is to get a group of people who are fully mingled with Him to be His universal expression and mutual dwelling place. The entire Bible reveals God in His Trinity working toward this goal. We see the Triune God reaching man, then bringing man back into Himself. In the Old Testament He was triune when He made man and dealt with man. In the Gospels He actually became a man—Jesus Christ. The Lord Jesus was the first man mingled with God. But God wanted many more such men, so in Acts we see Him as the Spirit propagating Himself into tens of thousands of believers. The Epistles show us the development of these believers into the church, the Body of Christ. In Revelation we see the final product, the ultimate consummation, of the Triune God's dispensing—the New Jerusalem. It is the enlargement and fullness of the lampstand, the church, and the vine tree. It is the ultimate mingling of humanity and divinity, the coinherence of God and man. This fulfills Genesis 1:26. The Bible ends the way it begins. It begins with God's image for His expression, and it ends with a vast, immense, splendid corporate expression. This is our eternal destination and the Triune God's eternal purpose. This is according to what the Father has planned, what the Son has accomplished, and what the Spirit is applying. What a plan! What an accomplishment! What an application! Praise the Triune God!

Questions

1. What is the relationship between the Triune God and the church?

2. Which verses substantiate that the church has the appearance of God? Explain.

3. Write a prophesy on the New Jerusalem being the ultimate consummation of the dispensing of the Triune God.

Quoted Portions from (Lee/LSM) Publications

1. *Life-study of Revelation,* pp. 89-93.

2. *Life-study of John,* pp. 401-402, 606-609, 611-612.

3. *The Basic Revelation in the Holy Scriptures,* pp. 68-69, 118, 120-124, 135.

4. *The Vision of God's Building,* pp. 223-224.

5. *The Divine Dispensing of the Divine Trinity,* pp. 144-146.

Lesson Thirteen

CHRIST'S PERSON AND WORK

Scripture Reading

Col. 1:17; Isa. 9:6; Rom. 9:5; Matt. 4:4a; Acts 2:22;
1 Tim. 2:5; Heb. 1:2, 10; Jn. 1:3; Col. 1:15;
John 1:14; Heb. 2:14

Outline

I. Christ being God

II. Christ being man

III. Christ being the Creator

IV. Christ being a creature

V. Christ's work

Text

In the next twelve lessons we will see who Christ is and the work He accomplished. This is what we call the Person and work of Christ. Many people throughout history have not been clear about this matter, so they have developed many heresies (wrong teachings) about Christ's Person and work. Christ is the central figure in God's economy for the accomplishment of His eternal purpose. We must spend some time to study this great truth of the Bible. The Bible is the foundation of all our beliefs. We can never deviate from what it says. Lessons Thirteen through Twenty-Four present the major points about Christ and His work which we see from the pure revelation of the Bible.

I. CHRIST BEING GOD

The first major point about Christ is that He is God, the God of eternity. We should not think that Christ did not exist before His birth at Bethlehem two thousand years ago. For you and me, birth was the beginning; but the Bible tells us that Christ existed before all things (Col. 1:17). Isaiah 9:6 tells us that the One born in the manger was the mighty God and the eternal Father. John 1:1 and 14 tell us that Christ was the Word in the beginning (in eternity past) and that this Word was God. Romans 9:5 says He is "the Christ, who is over all, God blessed forever."

Even in the Old Testament, Christ came to His people several times in the form of a man. On one occasion He ate a meal with Abraham (Gen. 18:1-33); on another occasion He wrestled with Jacob (Gen. 32:24-30); and on still another He appeared walking in the midst of a blazing furnace with three of His chosen people (Dan. 3:23-25). Although Christ is not specifically mentioned, we know it was He since He is the expression of God (John 1:18). God dwells in unapproachable light and no one has ever seen Him (1 Tim. 6:16), but in Christ He can be seen. Jacob even wrestled with Him! All of these instances are mysterious. We cannot explain how they were possible. This is why in one of His appearings He said His name is "wonderful" (Judg. 13:18, in Hebrew), which means that it is beyond our ability to understand. Some confused people believe that Christ was a man who later became God. This is heretical; the Bible does not say this. The Bible tells us that Christ is God from eternity past to eternity future.

II. CHRIST BEING MAN

The Bible also reveals to us that Christ is not only God but a man as well. Throughout the four Gospels, Christ called Himself "the Son of Man." When Satan came to tempt Him in the wilderness, Christ replied that man shall not live on bread alone (Matt. 4:4a). In Acts 2:22, Peter calls Him "Jesus the Nazarene, a man demonstrated by God to you." First Timothy 2:5 says, "For there is one God and one Mediator of God and men, the Man, Christ Jesus." Hallelujah, He is so wonderful! He is both God and man. In previous lessons we saw that Christ is the complete God, the Triune God. In later lessons we shall see that He is also a genuine man. This is why Christians have called Him the "God-man."

III. CHRIST BEING THE CREATOR

God is the Creator of all things (Gen. 1:1; 2:1-3). Since Christ is God, He surely is also the Creator. This fact is clearly revealed in the Scripture: "And, You in the beginning, Lord, have founded the earth, and the heavens are the works of Your hands" (Heb. 1:10). "All things came into being through Him, and apart from Him nothing came into being which has come into being" (John 1:3). "Through whom are all things, and we through Him" (1 Cor. 8:6). "Because in Him were all things created in the heavens and on the earth, the visible and the invisible, whether thrones or lordships or rulers or authorities; all things have been created through Him" (Col. 1:16). "Through whom [the Son] also He [God] made the universe" (Heb. 1:2). These verses clearly tell us that Christ is the Creator of all things; all things have been created and have come into being through Him.

IV. CHRIST BEING A CREATURE

Man is a creature (Gen. 1:27; Acts 17:26). Since Christ is a man, surely He is also a creature. This is revealed in Colossians 1:15, which says the Son is "Firstborn of all creation." This verse tells us in plain words that Christ is created because it says that He is the Firstborn of the creation, the First of all creatures. Revelation 3:14 also tells us He is created. In this verse Christ calls Himself "the beginning of the creation of God." He is the chief of the creation, the First One of all creatures.

Some people teach that Colossians 1:15 says that Christ is the Firstborn *before* all creation and that He is thus not a creature. But this is *not* what the Bible says. It says that Christ is the Firstborn *of* all creation. If you are the first-ranked student of your class, aren't you still part of your class? So Christ is part of the creation. He is a creature.

Christ is a creature because He became "flesh" (John 1:14), took part of "blood and flesh" (Heb. 2:14), was born a "child" (Isa. 9:6), and became a "man" (1 Tim. 2:5). "Flesh," "blood and flesh," "child," and "man"—these surely indicate creatures. Are not "flesh" and "blood and flesh" created things? Are not "child" and "man" created things? Of course they are! Therefore, since Christ became these things, how can we say that He is not a creature? If we acknowledge that Christ is a man, then we must admit that He is a creature. If we deny that He is a creature, then we deny that He is a man. People have been wrong throughout the centuries, but the Bible has never been and never will be wrong. We should not change the eternal Word of God to make it fit our thinking. Our concepts must line up with the truth of the Bible.

V. CHRIST'S WORK

It is crucial to see the Person of Christ because all of His work depends upon who He is. Christ can be our Savior because He is such a wonderful Person—He is God, the Creator, and a man, a creature. He could die as the Lamb of God for our sins because He is a man. His work of redemption is eternal in time and space because He is the eternal God. As God He can also put His divine life into us that we could fulfill His eternal purpose. Hallelujah for such a Christ! Praise Him for who He is and for the work He has accomplished!

Questions

1. What is a heresy?

2. Why is it heretical to say that Christ was a man who later became God?

3. Which verses show that Christ is the creator?

4. Which verses show that Christ is God?

5. Which verses show that Christ is a creature?

Quoted Portions from (Lee/LSM) Publications

1. *Concerning the Person of Christ,* pp. 19-47.

Lesson Fourteen

CHRIST'S INCARNATION

Scripture Reading

Matt. 1:20-23; Luke 1:32, 35; 2:21-24; Matt. 1:1; 9:6;
Rom. 8:3; 2 Cor. 5:21; Heb. 4:15; Col. 2:9; John 1:1, 14

Outline

I. As God
  A. Christ being God incarnated
  B. Christ being the Son of God
II. As man
  A. Christ being man
  B. Christ being the Son of Man
  C. Christ becoming flesh yet without sin
III. Christ being the mingling of God and man

Text

Incarnation is the first major step that Christ took to accomplish God's purpose. When we say God was incarnated we mean that God became a man; He took on flesh and blood. This was a tremendous event, the greatest in all of human history. The mighty God who existed in eternity became a lowly man in time. Christ did this not only to become our Savior, but more importantly to bring God into man, divinity into humanity. The more you consider Christ's incarnation the more you will be amazed. That little baby born in Bethlehem was the God of the whole universe! A proper realization of Christ's incarnation is the first and crucial step for our understanding of the Person and work of Christ.

I. AS GOD

A. Christ Being God Incarnated

The descriptions of Christ's conception and birth in Matthew and Luke clearly indicate that He is God Himself.

Matthew 1:20-23 says, "For that which is begotten in her is of the Holy Spirit. And she will bring forth a Son, and you shall call His name Jesus, for He shall save His people from their sins. Now all this took place that what was spoken by the Lord through the prophet might be fulfilled, saying, Behold, the virgin shall be with child and shall bring forth a Son, and they shall call His name Emmanuel, which being interpreted is, God with us."

In this passage there are three main points which strongly prove that our Lord Jesus is God Himself:

1) He was born through the impregnation of the Holy Spirit. The Holy Spirit is God Himself. Hence, because Jesus was born through the impregnation of the Holy Spirit, it means that He was God incarnated. The Holy Spirit is the essence of the Triune God (John 4:24). Therefore Jesus' essence was God. This agrees exactly with John 1:1 and 14, which say that He is God who became flesh.

2) God ordained His name to be called Jesus. "Jesus" in Greek is equivalent to "Joshua" in Hebrew (Num. 13:16; Heb. 4:8), which means "Jehovah Savior." This tells us that this Jesus is Jehovah God who became our Savior. Hence, He is God Himself. In the Old Testament He was only Jehovah. But praise the Lord, through incarnation He became Jesus, Jehovah our Savior!

3) God not only ordained His name to be Jesus, but men also called Him by the name Emmanuel. Emmanuel means "God with us." This also indicates that He is God. The One who became flesh and dwelt among men is God with men.

B. Christ Being the Son of God

When Jesus was to be conceived, God sent the angel Gabriel who said, "He will be great, and will be called, Son of the Most High...the holy thing which is born will be called, Son of God" (Luke 1:32, 35). Throughout the Gospels, Jesus is called the Son of God (Matt. 3:17; 14:33; 16:16; 27:54; John 1:34, 49). This title shows that the Lord is divine and that He is equal to God (John 5:17-18). Because of these points we should have no question that Christ was God incarnated.

II. AS MAN

A. Christ Being Man

The other side of the Lord's incarnation is that it occurred through Mary, a human virgin. This gave Jesus the human essence. He was one hundred percent man. He was God who had become a man. But He did not become a man suddenly. He stayed in a woman's womb like any other baby. Imagine that! God was confined in a woman's womb for nine months! Then He was born and brought up like any other Jewish child (Luke 2:21-24). Everything was done according to the ordinary human way, proving He had definitely become a man.

B. Christ Being the Son of Man

Although He was the Son of God, many times Jesus called Himself "the Son of Man" (Matt. 8:20; 9:6; 26:64; John 1:51; 3:13; 6:27). Matthew 1 gives the genealogy (family tree) of Jesus Christ. He is the Son of Abraham and the Son of David (Matt. 1:1). Therefore, Jesus was a genuine man.

C. Christ Becoming Flesh Yet Without Sin

Although the Lord became flesh, He was without sin. Christ was made in "the likeness of the flesh of sin" (Rom. 8:3), but He did not participate in the sin of the flesh. All of Adam's descendants have inherited Adam's sinful nature (Rom. 5:12,19); everyone is born in sin in Adam. This is why the Lord's virgin birth is very important. Although the Lord had the *likeness* of Adam, He did not inherit the *sinful nature* of Adam. He was not born in Adam. He was conceived of the Holy Spirit in the virgin Mary. As we shall see in a later lesson, it was necessary for Christ to know no sin (2 Cor. 5:21) and to be without sin (Heb. 4:15) in order for Him to accomplish redemption.

III. CHRIST BEING THE MINGLING OF GOD AND MAN

The incarnation of Jesus means more than the birth of a Savior. For four thousand years after Adam was created, God was God, and man was man. Yes, man had something to do with God, and God sometimes made contact with man, yet the two remained separate. However, when Christ was born as a man, a strange and wonderful event took place—God was brought into man and thereby formed a mingling of divinity with humanity. Jesus was God *and* He was man; He was a God-man.

Because He was conceived of the Holy Spirit, Jesus has the divine essence; and because He was conceived in a human virgin, Jesus has the human essence. Therefore, He is a Person with two essences—the divine and human—mingled together. It is unbelievable to our natural mind that the Almighty God would one day mingle Himself with man. But remember what God's eternal purpose is—God wants to get into man so that man would fully express God. This is just mingling. If Adam had eaten of the tree of life, he would have been a God-man, a man fully one with God. He would have been not just a good man but a God-man. Although Adam failed, Christ, through His incarnation, became the very first man to be mingled with God. Praise the Lord! The Lord Jesus was the Triune God embodied in a man. All the fullness of the Godhead dwelt in Him bodily (Col. 2:9).

"In the beginning was the Word...and the Word was God....and the Word became flesh" (John 1:1, 14). Never in the history of the universe had such a thing taken place. You should be very impressed with the great significance of the incarnation. It was so great that it caused an army of excited angels to burst forth from the heavens and praise God (Luke 2:8-14). Four thousand years after man's fall, God became Jesus (Jehovah our Savior) and Emmanuel (God with us). Hallelujah! God with us! Christ's incarnation inspired Charles Wesley to write a wonderful hymn. The first two stanzas follow.

> 1   Hark! the herald angels sing,
>   "Glory to the newborn King;
>   Peace on earth, and mercy mild;
>   God and sinners reconciled."

> Joyful, all ye nations, rise,
> Join the triumph of the skies;
> With angelic hosts proclaim,
> "Christ is born in Bethlehem."
> (Repeat the last two lines)

> 2 Christ, by highest heav'n adored,
> Christ, the everlasting Lord:
> Late in time behold Him come,
> Offspring of a virgin's womb.
> Veiled in flesh the Godhead see,
> Hail th' incarnate Deity!
> Pleased as man with man to dwell,
> Jesus our Immanuel.
> (Repeat the last two lines)

> (*Hymns*, #84)

God is no longer just God—He is God in man. God has been brought into man; divinity is mingled with humanity. What an incarnation!

Questions

1. What verses prove that Jesus was begotten of the Holy Spirit?

2. What does the title "Son of God" reveal?

3. What does the title "Son of Man" reveal?

4. Why is it so important for Christ to have flesh and blood yet to be without sin?

Quoted Portions from (Lee/LSM) Publications

1. *Life-study of John*, pp. 31-32.

2. *Life-study of Romans*, p. 186.

3. *Christ as the Reality*, pp. 40-41, 43-44.

4. *Life-study of Second Corinthians*, pp. 334-335.

5. *The Four Major Steps of Christ*, p. 6.

6. *Life-study of Luke*, pp. 5-6.

Lesson Fifteen

CHRIST'S HUMAN LIVING

Scripture Reading

John 1:45; Matt. 13:54-56; 9:10-11; John 4:6-7; 11:33, 35;
Luke 2:51; Mark 10:45; Matt. 11:29;
John 6:57; 5:30; Matt. 12:28; 2 Tim. 2:22

Outline

I. Christ being a genuine man
II. Christ being the perfect and finest man
  A. Obedient
  B. Serving
  C. Having no appearance of evil
  D. Having the finest personality
III. Divinity expressed through humanity
IV. Living by the Father and by the Holy Spirit
V. The proper humanity for the church

Text

We saw that through incarnation the mighty God became a man. Jesus was the Triune God manifested in the flesh. From His birth to His death the Lord lived on the earth for about thirty-three and a half years. The Lord's life described in the four Gospels shows us that He lived as a genuine man. Furthermore, His human living was perfect, without flaw. His living was according to the finest and highest standard. In this lesson we will see how Christ's humanity is the pattern for our own human living.

I. CHRIST BEING A GENUINE MAN

We saw previously how Christ's incarnation shows that He was a genuine man. His childhood and older years also prove that He was indeed a man. As a baby, Jesus was circumcised, named, and offered to God on His eighth day.

Jewish law required this for all Jewish boys. Philip saw Him as "the son of Joseph, from Nazareth," a real man (John 1:45). His own countrymen called Him "this man." They knew Him as "the carpenter's son," with a "mother," "brothers," and "sisters" (Matt. 13:54-56). These facts strongly prove that He is a man, not a bit different from an ordinary man. He ate with men (Matt. 9:10-11; Luke 7:36; John 12:2). He, "being wearied from the journey" and being thirsty, asked a woman for a drink (John 4:6-7). He "wept" as did those who were present at that time (John 11:33, 35). All these actions prove that He is a man.

II. CHRIST BEING THE PERFECT AND FINEST MAN

On one hand He was ordinary, but on the other hand He was unique. Every area of Jesus' human living was absolutely proper and perfect.

A. Obedient

Luke tells us that when Jesus was twelve years old, He knew how to care for His Father's will and yet at the same time be subject to His natural parents. He explained to His parents why He stayed in the temple but was still subject to them. He asked, "Did you not know that I must be in the things of My Father?" (Luke 2:49). Yet verse 51 says that He went with them and was subject to them. Some young people may say, "I am for God!"; but at home they are disobedient to their parents. This is not the fine, balanced humanity of Jesus.

B. Serving

In Mark 10:45 the Lord said, "The Son of Man did not come to be served, but to serve." Many people, especially some of the young people living at home, want to be served, but they never serve. They do not clean the house; they do not wash the dishes; they do not take care of their clothing; they do not even make their beds; they do not do anything. They just like to eat, sleep, and have a good time. This is not the humanity of Jesus. The humanity of Jesus is one to serve, not to be served. We do need such a spirit to serve others diligently.

C. Having No Appearance of Evil

In His ministry, the Lord contacted many kinds of people. Although He cared very much for their salvation, He always contacted them in a way which gave no appearance of evil. In John 3, Jesus was willing to meet with an elderly religious man in the middle of the night. But in chapter 4, when He spoke to a woman, He did it in broad daylight, in a very open and public place. He was very careful not only to avoid evil, but also to avoid the mere *appearance* of evil. He was more than proper when He dealt with members of the opposite sex. This kind of proper humanity is very much disregarded and even ridiculed in today's society. As a result, many young people have fallen into the damaging trap of immorality.

D. Having the Finest Personality

The Lord's personality was the finest. He was meek and lowly in heart (Matt. 11:29). He did not say that He was meek and lowly in appearance, but in heart. He was so meek that even little children could come to Him (Matt. 19:14). He was so lowly that even a despised, sinful woman could come and weep at His feet (Luke 7:38-39). He was so gentle that John, the disciple, could recline on His bosom during a meal together (John 13:23). Yet He overturned the tables of the evil money-changers in the temple (Matt. 21:12-13). He also knew when to rejoice and when to weep. He rejoiced in the Father's will (Luke 10:21), but He wept over the condition of God's people (Luke 19:41). In all things this man Jesus was so fine and balanced.

III. DIVINITY EXPRESSED THROUGH HUMANITY

We would need many lessons to consider every aspect of Jesus' life. The more we read about Him the more attracted to Him we should be. How could anyone have such a perfect human living? Only by being a God-man. The Lord Jesus was not just a good man; He was a man filled with God. His divinity was expressed through His humanity. This is why we are so struck by the fineness, loveliness, and balance of His humanity. His life cannot be imitated. In order to live the way Jesus did, you must be filled with God. God's purpose is that man would express God. So He made Adam in His own image and intended that he should eat of the tree of life. If Adam had done so, he would have been a man mingled with God and would have expressed God.

The Gospel of Luke shows us many instances in which the Lord's divinity was expressed in His human qualities. In 7:11-17 we see the Lord showing pity to a weeping mother by raising up her dead son. Verse 12 says, "Now as He came near the gate of the city, behold, one who had died was being carried out, the only son of his mother, and she was a widow; and a considerable crowd from the city was with her." This situation was very sad, and no one could do anything to comfort the grieving widow. First she had lost her husband, and now she had lost her only son.

Luke 7:13-15 says, "And seeing her, the Lord had compassion on her, and said to her, Do not weep. And approaching, He touched the coffin, and those carrying it stood still. And He said, Young man, I say to you, arise! And the dead man sat up and began to speak; and He gave him to his mother." Here we see the Lord's compassion in His speaking to the widow and touching the coffin. Would you like to touch a coffin with a dead person in it? The Lord was moved to do this by His human compassion. Then His divinity was expressed through that human compassion by raising the young man from the dead. Here we see that Jesus, the God-man, was full of the highest humanity with divinity.

IV. LIVING BY THE FATHER AND BY THE HOLY SPIRIT

The Lord Jesus lived His human life fully by the Father (John 6:57). Although He was God in the flesh, He never took the position of God. He lived as a man for God and with God. In the Gospel of John, Jesus said, "I can do nothing from

Myself;...I do not seek My own will, but the will of Him who sent Me" (5:30); "My teaching is not Mine, but His who sent Me" (7:16); "I do not seek My glory" (8:50); "I always do the things that are pleasing to Him" (8:29b); and "I and the Father are one" (10:30).

The Lord Jesus worked not by His own strength but by the Holy Spirit. He said in Matthew 12:28, "I by the Spirit of God cast out demons." In Luke, He was full of the Spirit, led by the Spirit, and came in the power of the Spirit (4:1; 4:14). From these points, we see that the Lord's human living was fully in God, by God, with God, and for God.

V. THE PROPER HUMANITY FOR THE CHURCH

God wants a group of people who are filled with Him and express Him—just like the Lord Jesus. For this we must have the proper humanity, which is the basic structure and strength of the church. Satan tries to frustrate God's purpose by attacking man's humanity. He especially attacks the young people with immorality, drugs, and mental illness. These things can damage young people to the point that they become useless for God's expression. We should not be ignorant of the enemy's tactics. Too many young people have been ruined and even killed by drugs and alcohol.

The Lord Jesus is living in us. You should sense the Lord objecting in your conscience when you begin to go too far in the things you do, the things you look at, and even the clothes you wear. Too many things in the world are designed to stir up people's lust—lust which Satan uses to damage humanity. In such matters you should not be too "spiritual," thinking that you can resist any temptation. Flee first! Then, seek the Lord with all them who call on Him out of a pure heart (2 Tim. 2:22).

The things we mentioned above must be more than clear to us. We must also realize that even our sloppiness and laziness can frustrate the Lord. You should sense the Lord objecting inside you when you throw your socks on the floor. It is easier to leave them there, but that is not the humanity of the God-man; that is your lazy self. What will your friends see when they visit your room? You may preach to them often about the Lord but they will only remember your messy room. How we need to enjoy the Lord's fine humanity! We, as the church, must be very different from today's constantly degrading society so that God can be expressed through the highest humanity.

Do not say, "I am not Jesus, I cannot be like Him. When I get older I will be better." No! Today, when you see that you are short of the standard of Jesus' humanity, you can open to Him, call on Him, and receive the Spirit. We cannot imitate the Lord's human living, but it can become ours by our taking Him in. We have said repeatedly that all that Christ is and has done is now in the life-giving Spirit. The Spirit today is the Spirit of the man Jesus. Not only is there divinity in the Spirit but even more there is the humanity of Jesus. This is the way to grow up into Christ in all things. You cannot be like Christ by imitation, but neither should you wait for the future to be like Him. Today is the day we can take Him in, live Him, and be "Jesusly" human. His highest, finest, and perfect humanity is our need today for the church life. Then God will be expressed through man for the testimony of Jesus. When we have such a living, others will be touched and will be attracted to the church.

Questions

1. Which verses prove that Jesus was a genuine man?

2. Which verses prove that Jesus was a perfect man?

3. Which verses show that Jesus lived by the Father's life and worked by the Spirit's power?

4. Explain how the highest, finest, and perfect humanity of Jesus is our present need for the church life.

Quoted Portions from (Lee/LSM) Publications

1. *Concerning the Person of Christ,* pp. 32-35.

2. *Christ as the Reality,* pp. 61-63, 69-78, 131-136, 153-159.

3. *Life-study of Luke,* pp. 68-69, 84-87, 129-130, 137-138.

4. *The Divine Dispensing of the Divine Trinity,* pp. 121-124.

5. *Life-study of Matthew,* pp. 410-411.

Lesson Sixteen

CHRIST'S CRUCIFIXION (1)

Scripture Reading

John 10:15; Heb. 12:2; John 1:29; Heb. 10:10-12; 9:28;
1 John 1:9; John 3:15; Heb. 2:14; Rom. 8:3;
2 Cor. 5:21; Heb. 4:15

Outline

I. The Lamb of God
II. The brass serpent

Text

Having lived an excellent human life for thirty-three and a half years after His incarnation, the Lord Jesus went to the cross. Crucifixion was the cruelest and most shameful way to die in those days. Yet we should not consider the Lord's death as a sad and tragic event. His death was the greatest and most wonderful death in the entire universe. In fact, the cross was the goal of Christ's incarnation and human living. On one hand the Lord was crucified by men, but on the other hand He went to the cross willingly in order to accomplish God's eternal purpose (John 10:15; Heb. 12:2). The cross was where He accomplished all His work of redemption so that man might be brought back to God.

You probably know that Christ was crucified for our sins. That is wonderful, but His death accomplished much more than that. In order to see this, we will take the next two lessons to look at five things that the Lord was when He died on the cross. The Bible tells us that He died as the Lamb of God, the brass serpent, the last Adam, the peacemaker, and the grain of wheat.

I. THE LAMB OF GOD

In John 1:29 when John the Baptist saw Jesus, he proclaimed to everyone: "Behold, the Lamb of God who takes away the sin of the world!" When man fell from God, God righteously had to require man to pay for those sins by the shedding of blood (by giving his life). But because of His love, God told the people they could substitute lambs and other cattle as sacrifices for their sins. By doing that, the people were spared from God's judgment.

Those Old Testament sacrifices were types (symbols) of Christ. God required those sacrificial lambs to be without spot or blemish (Exo. 12:5). We saw in Lesson Fifteen that He was indeed without spot or blemish. Christ came as the real Lamb of God. Before, the people had to offer the sacrifices over and over again. Their sins were not actually taken away; they were merely covered up (Heb. 10:11). But behold the Lamb of God who takes *away* our sins! Jesus offered Himself once for all (Heb. 9:28; 10:10, 12) for the forgiveness of all (Matt. 26:28). Because we have committed many sins, God requires the shedding of our blood. But Christ shed His blood for us. By believing in the Lord Jesus, we are completely forgiven of our sins and are freed from God's penalty of death!

God's intention is that we walk in holiness, but we still sin. Sinning can frustrate our fellowship with the Lord, but Christ's death as the Lamb of God fully takes care of this problem. "If we confess our sins, He is faithful and righteous that He may forgive us our sins and cleanse us from all unrighteousness" (1 John 1:9). God is absolutely righteous. Because Christ already died for us, He must instantly forgive us when we confess our sins. Afterward, we should not feel guilty. If we do, that is the Devil's lie. We should tell him, "Devil, you are a liar. I am cleansed by the Lamb's blood. I can fully enjoy the Lord!" This is how we can enjoy Christ's death as the Lamb of God.

II. THE BRASS SERPENT

When Adam ate of the forbidden tree in Genesis 3, Satan, the old serpent, injected his evil nature into man. Our nature was poisoned with Satan's nature and we became sinful, serpentine. This is why we often behave the way we do—like snakes. We also see this behavior all around us.

In the Old Testament, when the children of Israel sinned against God, many of them were bitten by serpents and died. When they cried out to Moses, the Lord told him to lift up a brass serpent on a pole. Everyone who looked at that serpent was forgiven, healed, and kept alive (Num. 21:4-9). In John 3:14 the Lord said, "As Moses lifted up the serpent in the wilderness, even so must the Son of Man be lifted up." This means that when the Lord Jesus was crucified on the cross, He was lifted up as the brass serpent. He died so that the serpent might be destroyed. As the Lamb, He died on the cross to take away our sin. But as the brass serpent, He died on the cross to destroy the old serpent, Satan, the Devil (Heb. 2:14).

The brass serpent had only the likeness of a serpent. It did not have the poisonous nature. In the same way, Christ was made in the likeness of the flesh of sin (Rom. 8:3) yet He had no sin (2 Cor. 5:21; Heb. 4:15). When Christ destroyed Satan, He also did away with the satanic nature in our flesh.

Satan is also the ruler of the world. The world is the system all around us which distracts us from God; it is the kingdom of darkness. Because Christ destroyed Satan, He also destroyed the world, his evil kingdom. As the brass serpent, Christ terminated Satan, our satanic nature, and the world.

That is Christ's finished work. We, however, still are bothered every day by our sinful flesh and the world. The world is always trying to draw us away from the Lord by stirring up the lust of our flesh. So, we must apply Christ as the brass serpent to our daily experience. Galatians 5:24 says that "they who are of Christ Jesus have crucified the flesh with the passions and the lusts." Romans 8:13 says that by the Spirit we can put to death the practices of our body.

Take watching television as an example. You might realize that many things on television are unhealthy and dirty for our minds. You may also know that it can be a waste of your time. Yet, you may have experienced an uncontrollable urge to watch it, even against your parents' wishes. That desire comes from the stirring up of the passions and lusts of your flesh. How can you be saved from it? You can be saved by turning to the Lord, who is the Spirit in your spirit. The Spirit contains everything Christ did, including His death as the brass serpent. When you call on Him, the Spirit comes with Christ's crucifixion to kill your flesh. This is how we put to death the practices of our body by the Spirit. This is how we terminate the lusts and passions of the flesh. You may fail sometimes—that is why we have the blood. But do not use that as an excuse to sin. We all need to call on the dear Lord's name to crucify the flesh. What a shame to the Devil! His efforts to use the world to attract our flesh will only cause us to call on the Lord even more! Hallelujah! Christ is the Victor!

Questions

1. What was the goal of Christ's incarnation and human living?

2. Why must Christ die as the Lamb of God as well as the brass serpent?

3. How can we apply what Christ has accomplished to our lives?

Quoted Portions from (Lee/LSM) Publications

1. *Stream Magazine Book Two,* p. 1491.

2. *Life-study of Mark,* p. 427.

3. *Life-study of First John,* pp. 73, 106-108.

4. *Life-study of John,* pp. 111-114, 229, 234-235.

5. *Life-study of Galatians,* pp. 251-252.

Lesson Seventeen

CHRIST'S CRUCIFIXION (2)

Scripture Reading

1 Cor. 15:45b; Rom. 6:6; Eph. 2:14-16;
John 12:24; Col. 2:14-15

Outline

III. The last Adam
IV. The peacemaker
V. The grain of wheat
VI. An all-inclusive death

Text

III. THE LAST ADAM

First Corinthians 15:45b says that Christ was the last Adam. When Adam was created by God, he represented the entire human race. Through Adam's race God intended to fulfill His eternal purpose. But Adam failed God to the uttermost; instead of taking in God, he took in Satan, and thus brought all of mankind into a fallen condition. Instead of expressing God, man began to express Satan. So God had to terminate the first man Adam and all of Adam's race, which includes you and me. God accomplished this through Christ's death on the cross. Christ was the last Adam; after Him there were no more Adams. God could then start a new race with Christ as its Head in resurrection.

Adam was also the head of the entire creation. He was given the rule over all the created things. The heavens and the earth were made for Adam, and Adam was made to contain Christ. But Adam fell and brought the whole creation down with him (Rom. 8:20-22). Without Christ, man, the heavens, and the earth are vain, without purpose. This fallen creation is what we call "the old creation." When Christ died as the last Adam He also terminated the entire old creation.

IV. THE PEACEMAKER

Christ also died as the peacemaker. One of the results of man's fall was division. God wanted man to express Him in oneness, but man became separated into many races, nationalities, and classes. There are often hatred and fighting among these groups—between black and white, German and French, rich and poor. The list is endless. The greatest difference is probably between the Jews and the Gentiles. The Jews have many ordinances (regulations) which separate them from other people. With all these differences, how could we all be one to express God? It is impossible. So Ephesians 2:14-16 tells us that on the cross Christ broke down all the dividing walls, abolished all the ordinances, and slew all the hatred between different people, races, and countries—even between you and your brother or sister. Christ is the peacemaker. He nailed all our differences to the cross.

Now in Christ there is no Jew or Gentile, rich or poor, black or white (Gal. 3:28; Col. 3:11). The cross terminated all such differences. If such differences still bother us, that shows we have not experienced enough of Christ's crucifixion. People always talk about ending wars and ending prejudice, but without the cross it is impossible to end anything. If you are fighting with someone, the best way to end the fight is to have both of you die. That may sound funny but it is the truth. When you are both dead, how peaceful you would be— there would be no more fighting! When Christ died as the peacemaker He crossed out everyone. We all died in Christ. This is why in the churches we can have people of every race, culture, and class. This is a glorious declaration of what the Lord Jesus did on the cross; by the cross we can be truly one. This oneness is real only in the Spirit. Therefore, whenever we have problems with people, we should turn to our spirit and allow the cross to terminate us.

V. THE GRAIN OF WHEAT

All of the first four aspects of Christ's death dealt with the negative problems such as sins and Satan. Now we must see that Christ also died as the grain of wheat. This is something on the positive side. In John 12:24, Christ described Himself as a grain of wheat: "Unless a grain of wheat falls into the ground and dies, it abides alone; but if it dies, it bears much fruit." When you plant a seed in the ground, that is a kind of death, a burial. But what happens after that? Life comes up! It even bears fruit to produce more seeds.

The life of a grain of wheat is hidden inside its outer shell. When the grain falls into the ground, the shell breaks and the life inside is released. In the same way, Christ's divine life was contained and concealed within the "shell" of His body. His death on the cross broke that shell so that His divine life could be released. His life was released so it could get into us! Before, He was the only God-man, a single grain. But through His death He has released His life. When we believed and called on the Lord Jesus, He came into us and we became His multiplication, the many grains! We became the many God-men just like Him. We can express God in our humanity as He did in His. How wonderful!

VI. AN ALL-INCLUSIVE DEATH

The Lord's crucifixion was neither a small nor simple event. It was an all-inclusive death. When Christ died, He accomplished a work much greater than the creation. That cross was the focus of the entire universe. Through it God cleaned up every negative thing and released His divine life! That One on the cross was not a simple man. Christ died as the Lamb of God to take away our sins and release us from God's judgment. He died as the brass serpent to crush Satan's head, crucify our serpentine nature, and destroy the world. He died as the last Adam to terminate Adam and the old creation. He died as the peacemaker to end all of man's differences and make peace. And He died as the grain of wheat to release His wonderful life into us.

If we had been at the Lord's crucifixion watching with "spiritual" eyes, we would have witnessed a tremendous scene. God was there working out His eternal purpose, and Satan and all the powers of hell were there battling, trying to frustrate Him. What a war it must have been! But Christ triumphed over them, putting them to open shame (Col. 2:14-15). Every negative thing in the universe was nailed to the cross and God's divine life was released. Hallelujah for Christ's work on the cross!

Questions

1. Explain the meaning and significance of Christ being the last Adam.

2. What does Ephesians 2:14-16 reveal to us regarding Christ's being the peacemaker?

3. Why did Christ use the death of a grain of wheat to illustrate His death?

Quoted Portions from (Lee/LSM) Publications

1. *Life-study of First Corinthians,* pp. 613-614.

2. *The Kernel of the Bible,* p. 124.

3. *The Spirit and Body,* pp. 20-21.

4. *Life-study of Ephesians,* pp. 721-724, 728-729.

5. *Stream Magazine Book Two,* pp. 1600-1601.

6. *Life-study of John,* pp. 315-317, 517.

7. *Life-study of Colossians,* p. 190.

8. *Life-study of Mark,* pp. 423-427, 432-433.

9. *The Economy of God,* p. 127.

Lesson Eighteen

CHRIST'S DEATH AS A GOD-MAN

Scripture Reading

Rom. 3:23; 6:23; Heb. 9:22; 2:14; 4:15; 1 Pet. 1:19;
Heb. 9:12; Matt. 27:46; 3:16-17; 1 Pet. 3:18

Outline

I. Died as a man
  A. Acquired man's blood
  B. Was without sin
II. Died as God
  A. For an eternal redemption
  B. To give eternal life
III. Heresies concerning Christ
IV. Christ being God essentially and having the Spirit economically

Text

Man's fall created a great dilemma for God. Man was the very center of God's desire, made to express Him. Yet because of man's sin, God's righteousness required man to be condemned. In this lesson we will see that God's solution to His dilemma is marvelously perfect and complete. The Lord Jesus is the unique Person who was qualified to die for our redemption.

I. DIED AS A MAN

A. Acquired Man's Blood

All men have sinned and the wages of sin is death (Rom. 3:23; 6:23). For man's sin, God required the payment of man's blood. Hebrews 9:22 says, "Without shedding of blood there is no forgiveness." This is why the Lord Jesus had to become a man. Man's blood was required, so God had to acquire such blood. God had no blood; but by His incarnation, He took on blood and flesh (Heb. 2:14). As the man Jesus, He could shed genuine human blood for our sake.

B. Was Without Sin

God had to become not just a man, but a *sinless* man. If Jesus had even one sin, He could never die for others' sins because He would have to die for His own. Therefore Christ knew no sin (2 Cor. 5:21; Heb. 4:15). He was made only in the *likeness* of the flesh of sin (Rom. 8:3). He was without spot or blemish (1 Pet. 1:19). From this we see that Christ was fully qualified to die for man. He could shed human blood and He could die for others because He had no sin.

II. DIED AS GOD

A. For an Eternal Redemption

Yet if Jesus were only a sinless man, we would still have a great problem. His death would be good for only one man; in fact, it would be good for only one sin. Let us explain. God requires man to die because of sin—even one sin. Suppose in your entire life you committed only one sin. As a sinless man, Jesus could die as a substitute for that sin. But if you were to sin again you would have to die for that second sin. Well, you know that you have sinned more than once in your life! How could one man, Jesus, die for all your sins and for all the sins of mankind? And how could it work for us two thousand years after His death?

We have pointed out before that although Christ became a man, He was still God. He was a genuine man, yet also the complete God. His being God added an eternal element to His redeeming blood. Hebrews 9:14 says that the Lord offered Himself up through the eternal Spirit. He has accomplished an eternal redemption for us (Heb. 9:12). Now Jesus' blood is effective for all men of all times. It can cleanse every sin of every man on the earth.

B. To Give Eternal Life

But redemption alone is not the goal of the Lord's work. His ultimate goal is to dispense His divine life into man. This is the aspect of Christ's death as the grain of wheat, which we saw earlier. Who could give man the eternal, divine life except God Himself? This is the second reason why Christ had to be God: only God could release the divine life into man. Praise the Lord Jesus! He is the unique God-man. No one could do what He did for us. As a man without sin, He was qualified to shed His blood for us. As God, He has made His death eternally effective. He has accomplished an eternal redemption and He has released the divine life of God into us.

III. HERESIES CONCERNING CHRIST

If we are clear about the previous points, we will realize how seriously wrong it is to say that Christ was not a real man or that He was not God. If either is true, then Christ's redemptive work would be utterly annulled. We would all perish.

Yet, as absurd as it is, there have been people throughout Christian history who have taught such heresies. Even today some say that Christ was God but not really a man. If that were true, then Christ could not shed human blood for man's sin. Others say that Christ was a man but not God, and that He died merely as a martyr. If that were true, His death would not be eternally effective and He could never put God's life into us. Still others say that Christ was neither God nor man but a third kind of being. This is as ridiculous as the other teachings. The Bible never gives any ground for such heresies. By now you should be very clear that the Lord Jesus was fully God and fully man. He was the complete God and a genuine man. He was a God-man. His death was the accomplishment of redemption for all mankind.

IV. CHRIST BEING GOD ESSENTIALLY AND HAVING THE SPIRIT ECONOMICALLY

Heretical teachings about Christ come from having an inadequate understanding of the Bible's description of Him. One verse that has especially confused people is Matthew 27:46. On the cross, right before His death, the Lord cried out, "My God, My God, why have You forsaken Me?" People have wrongly used this verse to say that Christ was not God since God forsook Him on the cross. They might also point out Matthew 3, where the Holy Spirit descended upon Jesus at His baptism. They ask, "If Jesus were God, why did He need the Holy Spirit to come upon Him?" This kind of question can be properly answered with what the Bible says.

Because the Lord was conceived of the Holy Spirit, He possessed the divine essence (Lesson Fourteen). You can say that He had the Holy Spirit as His essence, as part of His being. He was essentially God. Why then did the Holy Spirit descend upon Him at His baptism? This was necessary in order for the Lord Jesus to carry out His work. His baptism was the beginning of His three and a half year ministry on the earth. During that time He did many wonderful works such as preaching and performing many miracles. In the four Gospels He healed the sick and the crippled; He fed five thousand people with five loaves of bread and two fishes; He cast demons out of people and calmed the raging winds and seas; He even raised the dead. To do all those things He needed the authority and power of the Holy Spirit. We call this aspect of the Spirit "the economical Spirit." This is the Spirit that Jesus received at His baptism. He had the Spirit *essentially* for *life* at His birth and He received the Spirit *economically* for *power* at His baptism.

When Jesus was crucified on the cross, the sins of the human race were put on Him; He was made sin on our behalf (1 Pet. 2:24; 2 Cor. 5:21). The righteous God judged Jesus for man's sins. At that moment, God saw all the sins of the world on Jesus. The Holy God had to turn away, and the economical Spirit left Jesus. Thus Jesus cried, "My God, My God, why have You forsaken Me?"

Then we read in 1 Peter 3:18 that, on the cross, Christ was "being put to death in flesh, but made alive in spirit." When Jesus died on the cross for sinners, God left Him *economically*. But, according to this verse, God passed through crucifixion with Him *essentially*. This God-man was put to death in His human flesh, but made alive in His divine spirit. He had the essence of God from birth to death. His essential being never changed; in His essence He was still God and still man.

This should help us understand who Christ was on the cross: He was both God and man. We should have no doubt that the Lord Jesus was fully and uniquely qualified to die for mankind. Praise Him for His wonderful death as the God-man! Because of His accomplishment on the cross we are saved and are being saved. Hallelujah!

Questions

1. Explain the significance of Christ dying as a man. As God.

2. Discuss the consequences of the heretical teachings which state that Christ is God but not man or man but not God.

3. Explain the meaning of the Lord's last words, "My God, My God, why have You forsaken Me?"

Quoted Portions from (Lee/LSM) Publications

1. *Life-study of Mark,* pp. 413-419, 422-423.

2. *Life-study of First John,* pp. 69-70.

3. *Concerning the Person of Christ,* pp. 5-12.

Lesson Nineteen

CHRIST'S RESURRECTION (1)

Scripture Reading

John 11:25; 1 Cor. 15:45b; Rev. 1:17-18;
John 10:17-18; Acts 2:32; Rom. 4:25; 10:9;
Heb. 7:16; Acts 2:24;
Heb. 2:14; John 12:31; 1 Cor. 15:54-55

Outline

I. God's vindication of and satisfaction with Christ's person and work
II. The victory of Christ's resurrection
   A. Over death and Hades
   B. Over Satan and the world

Text

Christ died to accomplish redemption and to clean up all the negative things in the universe. He did a complete job; nothing was left unfinished. After His crucifixion and burial He resurrected. Neither death nor the tomb could hold this One since He Himself is the resurrection (John 11:25). His life is a death-conquering and death-subduing life. It is even a death-swallowing life (1 Cor. 15:54): the more death it encounters the more living it becomes. Therefore the Lord Jesus says, "I am...the living One, and I became dead, and behold, I am living forever and ever, and I have the keys of death and of Hades" (Rev. 1:17-18).

This living One who went into death was both God and man. Even after His resurrection, He is still God and man. His resurrection is of tremendous significance. In this lesson we will see that Christ's resurrection is His vindication and victory.

I. GOD'S VINDICATION OF AND SATISFACTION WITH CHRIST'S PERSON AND WORK

On the one hand, Christ is God; as God He laid down His life and took it up again (John 10:17-18). On the other hand, this One is a man whom God raised from the dead (Acts 2:32; 3:15). The raising of the man Jesus Christ shows God's approval of His Person and work. From His youth Jesus found favor with God (Luke 2:52). God vindicated Christ's crucifixion by raising Him up from the dead. This means that all that Christ did was accepted and honored by God the Father.

In Adam we were condemned to die because the wages of sin is death (Rom. 6:23). But Christ died as our substitute: He fully paid the price for our sins. How do we know that God has accepted Christ's payment? His resurrection is our "receipt," which proves that God has fully accepted Christ's payment for our sins. Suppose a criminal is sentenced to a certain prison term. How do we know whether he has served his sentence? We know when he is released. Resurrection therefore ends death. By believing in Christ, we are no longer pitiful sinners. We are fully justified, approved by God according to His own standard of righteousness. Not only so, but, as the resurrected One, He is also in us to live for us a life that can be justified by God and is always acceptable to God. Therefore, Romans 4:25 says that Christ was raised because of our justification. In fact, for our salvation, the primary thing that we believe in is Christ's resurrection (Rom. 10:9).

II. THE VICTORY OF CHRIST'S RESURRECTION

Next to God, death is the most powerful thing in the universe. No one can turn death away. No one, that is, except the Lord Jesus. He is the only One who has gone into death and come out living, never to return to death. He is both God and resurrection (John 1:1; 11:25), possessing the indestructible life (Heb. 7:16). Since He is such an ever-living One, death is not able to keep Him. He delivered Himself to death, but death had no way to hold Him (Acts 2:24).

A. Over Death and Hades

The Lord Jesus was in the domain of death for three days. He took a good look at death and found it to be power-less to hold Him. So on the third day the Lord Jesus simply walked out of death. He might have said, "Death, I have finished my mission; you can do nothing with Me, and I am not afraid of you. Now is the time for Me to walk out of your domain. I am not in a hurry. I could stay here for another day if I wanted to, but now it is time to leave." He was not fearful of death, running away from the tomb; rather, He peacefully took the time to fold His burial clothes and put them in good order (John 20:7). What a testimony of His victory over death!

In His resurrection, the Lord Jesus also took away the authority of death and Hades. This is why in Revelation 1:18 the Lord says, "I have the keys of death and of Hades." Because man fell into sin, death came in and is now working on earth to gather up all of mankind. Death resembles a dustpan used to collect dust from the floor, and Hades resem-bles a trash can. Whatever the dustpan collects is put into the trash can. Thus, death is a collector and Hades is a keeper. Death and Hades tried their best, but they could not keep Christ in their domain. Praise the Lord, death is subject to Him and Hades is under His control. Hallelujah! Christ has the keys of death and Hades.

B. Over Satan and the World

Christ's resurrection is also a testimony of His victory over Satan and the world. In His crucifixion Christ dealt with Satan. Hebrews 2:14 says that "through death He might destroy him who has the might of death, that is, the Devil." Also, when the Lord spoke to His disciples of His coming crucifixion, He said, "Now is the judgment of this world; now shall the ruler of this world be cast out" (John 12:31). The Lord took care not only of Satan, but also of Satan's system, the world. After finishing such a great task on the cross, Christ came out of death and Hades triumphantly. But Satan and the world did not fare so well. Christ defeated them by

His death and left them in the grave. His resurrection is a demonstration of that victory.

Are you impressed by Christ's resurrection? He has overcome the strongest enemy—death. Sometimes you may feel as though you were dead and buried. But consider the Lord Jesus. He actually went into death and Hades, and came out triumphantly. Your situation can never be worse than what the Lord Jesus went through. This living One is now in your spirit. When you feel depressed and weak, do not pray that the Lord would make you strong. All you need to do is to boldly declare, "Christ is resurrected! He has overcome death and Hades. Praise Him, He is Victor!" After such a prayer, you will proclaim as the Apostle Paul did: "Death has been swallowed up in victory. Where, O death, is your victory? Where, O death, is your sting?" (1 Cor. 15:54-55). Praise the Lord! Death could not hold Christ; neither can it hold those who are in Him.

Questions

1. Discuss the significance of God raising Christ from the dead.

2. Explain why Christ was raised for our justification (Rom. 4:25).

3. Discuss the significance of Christ's victory over Satan, death, and the world.

4. What verses substantiate Christ's resurrection?

Quoted Portions from (Lee/LSM) Publications

1. *Life-study of First Corinthians,* pp. 583-586, 621-622.

2. *Life-study of Matthew,* pp. 821-822.

3. *Life-study of Romans,* pp. 75, 567-568.

4. *Life-study of John,* pp. 317-318, 535-537.

5. *Life-study of Revelation,* p. 111.

6. *The Economy of God,* pp. 130-131.

7. *The Kernel of the Bible,* pp. 138-139.

Lesson Twenty

CHRIST'S RESURRECTION (2)

Scripture Reading

John 17:1; Rom. 1:3-4; John 1:18; Acts 13:33; Heb. 1:5;
John 7:37-39; 1 Cor. 15:45b; 2 Cor. 3:17; John 20:17;
1 Pet. 1:3; Rom. 8:29; Heb. 2:11; John 12:24;
1 Cor. 10:17; Eph. 1:22-23

Outline

III. The glorification of Christ's divine life
IV. The designation of Christ's humanity
V. His transfiguration into the life-giving Spirit
VI. His producing of the church

Text

In the last lesson we saw two aspects of Christ's resurrection. First, Christ's Person and His redemptive work were fully vindicated and accepted by God. Second, Christ won a full victory over death, Hades, Satan, and the world. Let us see four more aspects of His wonderful resurrection.

III. THE GLORIFICATION OF CHRIST'S DIVINE LIFE

When Christ was on earth, He was God concealed within a physical body. Inwardly there was God, but outwardly there was the flesh. When others looked at Christ, they could not see anything special about this One (Mark 6:3; John 10:33). But through Christ's death and resurrection, the God who was concealed within Him was released and made known. This display is what we call Christ's *glorification*. This is what He was praying for just before His death when He said, "Father, the hour has come; glorify Your Son that the Son may glorify You" (John 17:1).

Suppose we have a flower seed. Although much beauty is in the life of that seed, how can that beauty be manifested? The seed has to die. If the seed falls into the earth, dies, and grows up, the full beauty within it will be manifested. That is its glory, the glorification of the life in the seed. Likewise, at one time God was confined within the flesh of the Lord. The Lord had to die so that God within Him might be released, manifested, and glorified in resurrection.

When Christ was in the flesh during His thirty-three and a half years on the earth, He was exactly like the flower seed. Although the Son of God was in Him, no one could recognize this easily. By being sown into death and growing up in resurrection, He blossomed—that is, the divine life within Him was fully displayed, glorified.

IV. THE DESIGNATION OF CHRIST'S HUMANITY

Romans 1:3 and 4 say: "Concerning His Son, Jesus Christ our Lord, who came out of the seed of David according to the flesh, and was designated the Son of God...out of the resurrection of the dead." In resurrection, Christ was designated the Son of God in His humanity. Before His incarnation, Christ, as a divine Person, was already the Son of God (John 1:18). He was the Son of God before His incarnation, and even Romans 8:3 says, "God sending His own Son." Since Christ was already the Son of God, why did He need to be designated the Son of God through resurrection? Because by incarnation He had put on the flesh, the human nature that had nothing to do with divinity. As a divine Person, Christ was the Son of God before His incarnation; but that part of Him which was Jesus with the flesh, born of Mary, was not the Son of God. That part of Him was human. By His resurrection, Christ has sanctified and uplifted His human nature, His humanity; He was designated out of this resurrection as the Son of God with this human nature. So, in this sense, the Bible says that He was begotten the Son of God in His resurrection (Acts 13:33; Heb. 1:5).

In His resurrection, Christ is still a man; as such He has been designated the Son of God. This is not an insignificant matter. The incarnation brought God into man, but the resurrection brought man into God. Because of the process Christ went through, a man has been brought into the Godhead. Yes, there is now a man in the Godhead! Christ in His human nature has been designated the Son of God.

V. HIS TRANSFIGURATION INTO THE LIFE-GIVING SPIRIT

Next we would like to see that in His resurrection Christ became a life-giving Spirit (1 Cor. 15:45b). Although the Lord Jesus was resurrected with a physical body, a body with flesh and bones (Luke 24:39), He was also resurrected spiritually. This means that in His resurrection He was transfigured into the Spirit (John 7:37-39; 1 Cor. 15:45; 2 Cor. 3:17). We cannot explain how He could both have a body and at the same time become the Spirit, but that is what the Bible says. This is a major point in the Bible. We see that Christ is sitting on the throne in the heavens with a physical body, yet at the same time, He is dwelling in us as the life-giving Spirit. God's economy is to dispense Himself into us. His death redeemed us, but without His resurrection He could not dispense His life into us. We were not only sinful, we were also dead (Eph. 2:1). As the Lamb of God, Christ can redeem us. But as the life-giving Spirit He can enliven us and regenerate us to become the children of God. Now, day after day, we can enjoy the rich supply of life that is in the Spirit. We can pray, call on His name, and pray-read the Word. Christ is now so available to us because of His resurrection. Christ's resurrection is not just a historical event; it is very much for our inward experience and enjoyment of Christ.

VI. HIS PRODUCING OF THE CHURCH

The death and resurrection of Christ were very productive steps in God's economy: He released His divine life and propagated (spread) Himself into many people to make them the church. According to the Gospel of John, prior to His resurrection, the Lord never called His disciples "brothers."

The most intimate term He used was "friends." But after His resurrection, His "friends" were regenerated to become His "brothers" (John 20:17; 1 Pet. 1:3). In the evening of the day of His resurrection, Christ came back to His disciples as the Spirit and breathed Himself into them to be their life. It was through His resurrection that the Lord was able to impart Himself as the life-giving Spirit into all His disciples. By receiving His life, they were regenerated and became His brothers. Therefore, in His resurrection, the only begotten Son became "the Firstborn among many brothers" (Rom. 8:29).

Through Christ's resurrection, the divine life of the Father has been imparted into us. Thus, we all have become sons of God and brothers of Christ. Praise the Lord that Christ, the God-man, is our elder Brother! He is not ashamed to call us His brothers (Heb. 2:11). What a wonder! Do you realize who you are? You are a brother of Christ! This is the same principle as that of the grain of wheat in John 12:24. The many brothers are the many grains of wheat, and these many grains are blended together to form the church. Therefore 1 Corinthians 10:17 tells us that "we who are many are one bread, one Body." The many grains have become one loaf, one Body. The one Body, of course, refers to the church as the Body of Christ (Eph. 1:22-23). The church is just the duplication and multiplication of Christ.

Praise the Lord for His resurrection! Many Christians speak a great deal about Christ's death on the cross, but rarely do they talk about Christ's resurrection. When they do, they only speak about how the Lord rose up from the grave. They consider His resurrection to be only a historical event that happened two thousand years ago. They celebrate it one day of the year. That is too shallow! In just two lessons we have seen some of the tremendous items of Christ's resurrection. We must be thankful for the wonderful riches that the Lord has shown us from His Word in these days. We encourage you to dig into these matters even more and to enjoy Christ as the resurrected One in us.

Questions

1. Explain how Christ's divine life was glorified.

2. Christ was the Son of God before His resurrection. Why does Romans 1:3-4 say that He was designated the Son of God out of the resurrection?

3. Which two verses clearly tell us that Christ is now the Spirit?

4. Why was Christ called the "only begotten Son" in John 1:18, but was called the "Firstborn" in Romans 8:29.

Quoted Portions from (Lee/LSM) Publications

1. *Life-study of John,* pp. 316-317, 546-549.

2. *Life-study of Romans,* pp. 18-23, 552-554, 570-571.

3. *Life-study of First Corinthians,* pp. 614-616.

4. *Life-study of Hebrews,* pp. 94-96.

Lesson Twenty-One

CHRIST'S ASCENSION

Scripture Reading

Eph. 4:8; Mark 16:19; Heb. 2:9; Phil. 2:9; Acts 2:36;
Rev. 1:5; Eph. 1:22; Acts 5:31; Rev. 19:16; Acts 7:55-56;
Rev. 2:1; 5:6; Heb. 4:14-15; 7:25

Outline

I. Being made Lord
II. Being made the Christ
III. The Lord's inauguration
IV. Christ's heavenly ministry
    A. Christ as Ruler
    B. Christ as Head
    C. Christ as our High Priest
V. Our cooperation

Text

After His resurrection, Christ ascended to the heavens to God the Father. This was the last major step of the process He went through. Ephesians 4:8 says He "ascended to the height." Christ is now at the highest place in the universe. Mark 16:19 says that the Lord was "taken up into heaven and sat at the right hand of God." To be seated at God's right hand means that Christ is at the place of greatest honor and highest authority. There He is crowned with glory and honor (Heb. 2:9), has been exalted far above all, and has received the name above all names (Phil. 2:9).

I. BEING MADE LORD

In His ascension, Christ was made the Lord (Acts 2:36), the Ruler of the kings of the earth (Rev. 1:5), as well as Head over all things (Eph. 1:22). This means that He is the Ruler of the universe, the authority on the throne of God's government. He is the landlord of the whole universe! This may not impress you that much. You might think that because Christ is God, the Creator, He already was the Lord and Ruler of the universe. But you must realize that the Christ who is Lord today is not just the Lord who created the universe. The Christ who is Lord today is God incarnated to be a man. In His resurrection and ascension He is still a man. So now, there is a man in the heavens, exalted and established as the Lord of the universe! It is easy for us to believe that the Creator God is the Lord. But can you believe that the man Jesus, the poor carpenter, is now on the throne over the entire universe? A little man from the small country village of Nazareth has been made Head over all things!

II. BEING MADE THE CHRIST

Acts 2:36 says that in His ascension Jesus was also made Christ. "Christ" means that He is God's Anointed One; He is the One appointed by God to accomplish God's plan. The Father sent the Son to do all the work of redemption and everything related to God's purpose. So, the Son is called Christ. But wasn't He the Christ before His ascension? Yes, He was, but not officially. In His ascension the Lord was officially made Christ.

III. THE LORD'S INAUGURATION

A good way to understand the Lord's ascension is to think of it as His *inauguration*. Whenever a new president is elected in the United States, he must be inaugurated. Before the inauguration he is the president, but not officially. There must be a public declaration, an inauguration, for him officially to become president. The ascension of Jesus is the same. He was the Christ and the Lord, but this was not official until His ascension. In fact, He was not even the official Savior until His ascension (Acts 5:31). Praise the Lord for His ascension! Jesus the little Nazarene is now the King of kings and Lord of lords (Rev. 19:16). When the President of the United States is inaugurated, thousands of people parade through Washington, D. C. Who knows how many angels paraded in the heavens when Jesus was inaugurated to be Lord of all!

IV. CHRIST'S HEAVENLY MINISTRY

The Lord Jesus surely had a fruitful life on the earth. We call His work on the earth His earthly ministry. Through incarnation, human living, death, and resurrection, the Lord fully accomplished the work of redemption. This is why we read many Bible verses which say that Christ sat down after His ascension. Because His earthly ministry was a tremendous success, He is sitting, resting at the right hand of God.

However, that is only one side of the story. Christ also has a great work to do from the heavens; He has a heavenly ministry. When Stephen was being stoned, he looked up into heaven and saw "Jesus *standing* at the right hand of God" (Acts 7:55-56). In Revelation 2:1 John saw the Lord *walking* in the midst of the seven golden lampstands. In Revelation 5:6 he saw the Lord as the Lamb *standing* in the midst of the throne. Do not think that Christ is sitting in the heavens with nothing to do! He is extremely active in His heavenly ministry. After being inaugurated into office He has important duties. Of the various offices into which He was inaugurated at His ascension, the three greatest are that He is Ruler of the kings of the earth, Head over all things to the church, and our great High Priest.

A. Christ as Ruler

As Ruler of kings, Christ is administrating (controlling and arranging) all the governments and events on this earth. The purpose of this administration, no doubt, is for the spreading of the gospel. By this means God's chosen ones are being gathered in. From studying world history we can see that the course of events has been arranged for the spread of the gospel. Our calendar, which is used all over the world, is based on the birth of Christ. Even atheistic countries like Russia and China use this calendar, thus implying that they are under Christ's sovereign ruling. According to Christ's calendar, we are in the year 1985. This date does not refer to the Roman Caesars or to the Russian Czars, but to Christ's birth. Our Christ is Ruler over the whole earth for the spread of His gospel!

B. Christ as Head

In addition to His sovereignty over the nations, Christ also exercises His headship. As Head over all things to the church, He works to gain His chosen vessels. Just consider one vessel, Saul of Tarsus. The book of Acts shows us how much the ascended Christ did to win Saul. Saul was a crucial vessel for God's move on the earth.

Do not think your salvation is a small thing. It was accomplished because the Lord Jesus exercised His rulership. He arranged that you should be born in the country in which you were born. Your place of birth was not accidental, but under His administration. You were born in the right country, the right town, the right family. At the right time He brought you to Himself. You may have been in America, China, Europe or South America. One day He arranged for you to be at a certain spot, and you repented, believed, and were saved. If you had been in Moscow, the opportunity to be saved and now to be reading this lesson might not have come to you. It was under the King's rulership that you got saved!

C. Christ as Our High Priest

The ascended Christ is also ministering to our inward need. In Old Testament times the high priest ministered to God on behalf of His people. Hebrews tells us that Christ is our great High Priest who can sympathize with our weaknesses (4:14-15). Because Christ became a man, He thoroughly knows our weak points and problems. But He is also God, constituted according to the power of an indestructible life (Heb. 7:16). Therefore He is able to take care of us in any situation (Heb. 7:25).

Surely every hour we need Him. From hour to hour we do not know what situations will confront us. Sometimes troubles come to us and we get anxious. Before we were saved, these worries were endless. But now, when anxious thoughts arise, we soon sense a soothing comfort, saying to us, "Why don't you pray? You don't need to worry." Christ has begun to intercede for us, and this is the effect it produces. Then we respond to Him, "Thank You, Lord. You bear my worries. All my cares are in Your hand." Just a few short words and the anxiety is lifted! We can enjoy Him. This is Christ's priestly intercession for us. It is unending. We should have many experiences of being reminded, comforted, strengthened, and even carried by our great High Priest.

V. OUR COOPERATION

Christ is more than qualified for the great offices He holds in His heavenly ministry. He is working day and night. He is controlling every event on the earth—from the rise and fall of nations to the teacher you get for English. All this is so that He can carry out God's great eternal purpose. Yet without our cooperation, the ascended Christ can do very little. He is our great Head but we are His Body. On earth, He can move only through us, His members. This is a very serious matter. Christ requires our cooperation.

He desires all men to be saved but He cannot save them unless we speak to them. In this respect, the almighty God cannot do anything unless we cooperate with Him. What a responsibility, but what a privilege! We can be those who allow God to move on the earth for the fulfillment of His eternal purpose! We are the V.I.P.'s of the universe. But we must be faithful to cooperate with Him.

Questions

1. How wonderful it is that Jesus was made Lord, Head over all things. Why?

2. How is the Lord's ascension His inauguration?

3. What are the three greatest offices to which Christ was inaugurated at His ascension? How does He minister in these offices?

4. As the Lord of all, can Christ do everything by Himself? Does He need help? Who are His helpers? How can they help?

Quoted Portions from (Lee/LSM) Publications

1. *The Experience of Life,* p. 337.

2. *Stream Magazine Book One,* p. 6.

3. *Stream Magazine Book Two,* pp. 1426-1430.

4. *Life-study of Revelation,* p. 38.

5. *The Heavenly Ministry of Christ,* pp. 2-4, 9-10, 13, 17, 20-23, 34-35, 52-55.

6. *Life-study of Hebrews,* pp. 175-176.

Lesson Twenty-Two

CHRIST AS THE ESSENTIAL
AND ECONOMICAL SPIRIT

Scripture Reading

Jn. 20:22; Acts 2:1-4; Rom. 8:10-11; 2 Cor. 13:5;
2 Tim. 4:22; John 6:63; Luke 24:49; Acts 1:4-5, 8;
Mark 16:15; 1 Cor. 12:13

Outline

I. The inward content and the outward equipment
II. The essential (inward) aspect
   A. Christ in us
   B. Christ as our life
   C. The content of the church
III. The economical (outward) aspect
   A. The baptism of the Holy Spirit
   B. The propagation of Christ
IV. Our experience of both aspects of the Spirit

Text

Christ has passed through a marvelous process. He has gone through incarnation, human living, crucifixion, resurrection, and ascension. Every item of that process was a further step in God's economy. That economy is to produce the church as the Body of Christ—the full, corporate expression of the Triune God and the mutual dwelling of God and man. As we pointed out in the previous lesson, Christ, the Head in heaven, needs His Body on the earth to coordinate fully with Him in order to carry out His purpose. We cannot do anything without Him but neither can He do anything without our cooperation. The crucial element of this coordination is that Christ is now the Spirit. As the Spirit, He can live in us and supply us inwardly; and at the same time He can empower us and work with us outwardly.

I. THE INWARD CONTENT
AND THE OUTWARD EQUIPMENT

Many Christians do not realize that on the day of resurrection the resurrected Christ came as the heavenly breath and breathed Himself into His disciples (John 20:22). This is one aspect of the formation of the church. Then, fifty days later on the day of Pentecost, the ascended Christ on the throne poured Himself out upon the disciples (Acts 2:1-4). This is another aspect. The breathing out of the holy breath on the day of resurrection was for *life*, and the pouring out of the Spirit on the day of Pentecost was for *power*. On the day of resurrection there was the "pneuma." That is the Greek word for "Spirit"; it also means "breath" or "air." But on the day of Pentecost there was the mighty wind. Air is for life and wind is for power. The Spirit of life, who is the resurrected Christ, is our content of life; the Spirit of power, poured out by the ascended Christ, is our outward equipment. Thus, we have the inward content of life and the outward equipment of power. The first is *essential* and the second is *economical*. These are not two Spirits, but are two aspects of the one Spirit. We must be very clear about these two aspects of Christ as the Spirit.

II. THE ESSENTIAL (INWARD) ASPECT

A. Christ in Us

Many Bible verses tell us that Christ is in us (Rom. 8:10; 2 Cor. 13:5; Gal. 2:20; Col. 1:27). He can live in us because He is the Spirit. Therefore other verses say that the Spirit is in us (John 14:17; Rom. 8:11; 1 Cor. 6:19; Gal. 4:6). When Christ was a man on the earth, He could not live inside anyone. Now, however, Christ is the Spirit (1 Cor. 15:45b; 2 Cor. 3:17). He is like the air that is around us; He can easily come into us. As the Spirit, the Lord regenerated us; our spirit is now born of the Spirit (John 3:6). Christ now dwells in our spirit (2 Tim. 4:22).

B. Christ as Our Life

It is by the Spirit that we enjoy Christ as our inward life.

He is the Spirit that gives life. In such a Spirit we enjoy Christ by reading His Word (John 6:63; 2 Tim. 3:16), calling on His name (1 Cor. 12:3), and praying (Jude 20). This is the eating, drinking, and breathing of Christ. This causes Christ to be dispensed into us as the Spirit for our living. We need physical food, water, and air to sustain our bodies. In the same way, we need to take in Christ as the Spirit to sustain our spiritual life. He is our living bread, living water, and living air. This is the Spirit of life for our *essential* being and living.

Although the Lord has entered into us, we cannot say that our entire being is filled with Him. We are still full of our old nature. Instead of expressing the Lord, we express selfishness, pride, rebellion, and many other things. We greatly need the inward sanctifying and transforming work of the Spirit.

The Spirit is the ultimate consummation of the processed Triune God. He is all-inclusive; He contains every item of the process that the Lord went through. He has the Lord's perfect human living, the killing element of the cross, and the resurrection power. As we enjoy such a Spirit, our being will begin to change. Christ's living will become ours, the negative things in us will be killed, and our life will be a life in resurrection.

C. The Content of the Church

When we enjoy Christ in this way, He becomes our inward content. He is the content of the church. The church is not a social club or just a group of people who meet together; it is the Body of Christ. To be His Body we must be full of His life. Suppose someone made a plastic model that looked exactly like your body. Would you call it your body? Of course not. In order for it to be your body it must be full of your life. As the Body of Christ, we need to be filled with Christ as our life. So Christ became the Spirit to dispense Himself as life into us.

III. THE ECONOMICAL (OUTWARD) ASPECT

A. The Baptism of the Holy Spirit

After His resurrection, Christ appeared to His disciples

and instructed them not to depart from Jerusalem, but to wait for the baptism of the Holy Spirit (Acts 1:4-5). He said, "But you shall receive power when the Holy Spirit has come upon you, and you shall be My witnesses...unto the remotest part of the earth" (Acts 1:8). According to His word, the Holy Spirit was poured out upon the Body on the day of Pentecost. This baptism of the Holy Spirit was not for life *essentially* but for power and authority *economically*. The disciples were already filled with the Spirit for life, but they needed to be "clothed with power from on high" for the work (Luke 24:49). This clothing is the "heavenly uniform" of the economical Spirit.

B. The Propagation of Christ

The authority and power of the Spirit were to equip the disciples for the Lord's work. The Lord had told them to "go into all the world and preach the gospel to all the creation" (Mark 16:15), and to be His witnesses unto the remotest part of the earth. Christ had gotten into some people in Jerusalem, but desired to get into thousands, even millions more. That would be His multiplication and spreading—His propagation for the producing of the churches over the entire earth. Clothed with the economical Spirit, the disciples went out to preach the gospel. On one day three thousand repented, and on another five thousand were saved! The Spirit was their life inwardly and their authority outwardly. This is why their work was so prevailing.

IV. OUR EXPERIENCE OF BOTH ASPECTS OF THE SPIRIT

Even Christ as a man experienced the two aspects of the Spirit: He was born of the Holy Spirit essentially, and also baptized with the Spirit economically for His ministry and work. Every believer in Christ should experience the same thing. God's desire is for a universal expression of Himself, a corporate man that is filled with His life and nature. To produce this expression, God has ordained that it be carried out by mortal men on the earth cooperating and coordinating with Him. What a monumental task! Yet, we are more than able; Christ went through a tremendous process for this purpose. Now we can enjoy and experience the life-giving Spirit as our life and life supply. By now we should be clear of the many ways that we can partake of the Spirit for our essential living. But in order to go out to preach Christ to others, we need the "heavenly uniform." How do we experience this economical aspect of the Spirit? We experience it by faith. The baptism of the Holy Spirit upon the Body in Acts was a once-for-all accomplishment. We do not need to wait for it. We have it already. First Corinthians 12:13 says that "in one Spirit we *were* all baptized into one body." Now we simply go out to preach confident of that fact. When we exercise our faith in this way we will find that hell, Satan, and the demons cannot prevail against our ministry. We will be clothed with the "uniform" of greatest authority. Our preaching of Christ will prevail to bring Christ into others.

Here we see a wonderful cycle for the propagation of the resurrected and ascended Christ. First, we are filled and nourished with Him essentially. Then, clothed with Him economically, we dispense Him to others that they may also enjoy Him as their life essentially. Our essential enjoyment of the Lord is so that we may work economically to spread Him into others. But what we dispense to others must be what we are filled with essentially. One aspect is for the other. We cannot do without either. Praise the Lord! Christ will get His Body on the earth in this way. Each day we need to take Christ as the Spirit as our life. Then, knowing that we have the Spirit as our "uniform," we should carry out God's work of spreading and multiplying Himself into others. We are well able to do it!

Questions

1. What does "essential" mean? What does "economical" mean?

2. How did Christ, as the Spirit, produce the church with both the essential and economical aspects?

3. When did the disciples first experience both aspects of the Spirit?

4. How can we experience both aspects of the Spirit?

Quoted Portions from (Lee/LSM) Publications

1. *The Kernel of the Bible,* pp. 158-159, 161-162, 165-169.

2. *The Baptism in the Holy Spirit,* pp. 3-7.

3. *Life-study of Mark,* pp. 570-572.

4. *The Spirit and Body,* pp. 42-44.

Lesson Twenty-Three

CHRIST'S SECOND COMING

Scripture Reading

Rev. 22:12, 20; Matt. 24:36;
Rev. 10:1; 14:4; Matt. 24:21-22; 2 Cor. 5:10;
Matt. 25:10; Rev. 2:26; 1:7; 14:14

Outline

I. The secret coming
II. The judgment seat of Christ
III. The open coming
IV. A warning

Text

The church has existed on the earth for nearly two thousand years. Christ now lives in millions of believers as the life-giving Spirit. At the same time, He is in the heavens as the Head over all things to the church. There Christ is administrating all the events in heaven and on earth for the building up of His Body. When the time is right, this Christ who is on the throne will begin His return to the earth. At the end of Revelation He says, "Yes, I come quickly" (22:20). The Lord's incarnation was His first coming. But this verse is about His second coming. Christ's second coming will begin the final stage of God's economy. It is a very important part of Christ's work.

The subject of Christ's second coming has confused Christians for hundreds of years. It is very complicated and has many events related to it. It would take us many lessons to explain properly all its details and events. However, there are two major aspects of the Lord's return that we must be very clear about: one aspect is His secret coming; the other is His open, or public, coming.

I. THE SECRET COMING

The day and the hour of the Lord's return no one knows, "but the Father only" (Matt. 24:36). At the proper time, Christ will begin to descend from the throne. This descent is hidden and secret. Revelation 3:3 and 16:15 both tell us that Christ will come as a thief and that we should be watchful. No thief comes openly or announces his coming. Revelation 10:1 says that Christ will be "clothed with a cloud." This means He will be wrapped up or concealed in a cloud. But some time before He leaves the throne, some overcomers will be raptured (taken up) to the throne. These overcomers are the believers on the earth who have kept themselves from the defilement (pollution) of worldly things. The Lord is their first and best love. These overcomers are called the "firstfruit" (Rev. 14:4). In any kind of harvest there is always some fruit that ripens first. That is the choicest fruit.

The rapture of the firstfruit signals the start of the "great tribulation" (Matt. 24:21-22). The great tribulation will be a three and a half year period of great suffering and persecution. Those days will be more terrible than anyone can imagine. The majority of Christians who are alive at that time will have to go through all or part of this great tribulation. These are the Christians who did not fully give themselves to be separated from the world in order to be filled up with Christ. The great suffering of this time will help mature these saints, just as the hot sun helps to ripen a crop. But being saved out of the great tribulation will be a great reward for the raptured overcomers. In Revelation 3:10 the Lord says, "Because you have kept the word of My endurance, I also will keep you out of the hour of trial which is about to come on the whole inhabited earth, to try them who dwell on the earth."

II. THE JUDGMENT SEAT OF CHRIST

Before the end of the great tribulation, Christ will have descended to a place in the air to set up His judgment seat. All the living Christians who still remain on the earth will be raptured to the air. This is what we call the general harvest.

All the dead Christians will also be raised to meet the Lord. Second Corinthians 5:10 says that we must all stand before the judgment seat of Christ to receive either reward or punishment for the things we have practiced during our life. We will be judged in two areas: maturity in life and faithfulness in service (Matt. 25:1-30). To be mature in life means that the Christ who came into us has fully grown up till every part of our soul is filled with Him. That means our thoughts, our love, and our choices are filled with Christ. We have denied ourselves and taken the cross that Christ as the life-giving Spirit might fill these parts.

To be faithful in service means to be faithful in outward works. These include preaching the gospel for others to be saved, serving in the church, and functioning in the church meetings. To meet the Lord, we must be proper and balanced in these two areas—life essentially and service economically.

Those believers who are found to be mature and faithful will receive a great reward. With the overcomers, they will participate in the wedding and wedding feast of Christ the Lamb. Christ will be the groom and the saints will be the bride. This will all take place in the air before Christ's open coming. "Blessed are they who are invited to the marriage dinner of the Lamb" (Rev. 19:9). Matthew 25:10 says, "The bridegroom came, and those who were ready went in with him to the marriage feast, and the door was shut." What a tremendously joyful time that will be! This enjoyment will continue through the millennial kingdom where the saints will rule as co-kings with Christ over all the nations (Rev. 2:26; 20:4).

Those who are neither mature nor faithful will receive a punishment. They will not be eternally lost, but they will be disciplined for a thousand years. During this time these believers will mature to be proper sons of God (Heb. 12:5-10). Although the result will be maturity, the process will not be by grace. The Bible describes that time as the "outer darkness" where there is weeping and gnashing of teeth, suffering ruin, being burned by fire, and being beaten with many stripes (Matt. 22:13; Heb. 10:39; 1 Cor. 3:15; Luke 12:45-48).

III. THE OPEN COMING

After the wedding, from that place in the air, Christ will openly descend to the earth, no longer as a thief but rather with power and great glory. He will be seen by all the tribes of the holy land (Rev. 1:7; Matt. 24:27, 30). In His secret coming to the air He will be *clothed with* the cloud, but in His open coming to the earth He will be *on* the cloud (Rev. 14:14). When Christ comes openly, He will come with the overcoming saints to fight against Antichrist and his armies which will be gathered against Israel at a place in the Middle East called Armageddon. There the Lord will exterminate the evil worldly forces and will save Israel. Satan will be bound and the thousand-year kingdom will begin.

IV. A WARNING

Many Christians today are taught that when the Lord returns, all the believers will be instantly raptured to live "happily ever after" with the Lord. This is not what the Bible teaches. Such teachings have "drugged" the Christians, causing them to live loosely and carelessly. Many indulge in worldly and fleshly pleasures. In light of the truth we have seen from the Word of God, we must be warned against this kind of living.

You may be curious about all the details of the Lord's return, but the most important thing is to pick up the principle of His second coming as a warning. The principle is that we must be mature so that we may escape the coming great tribulation and receive a reward rather than a punishment at the judgment seat of Christ. This requires us to daily turn our hearts to the Lord to love Him, to be filled with Him, and to serve Him. When you are tempted by the worldly things, remember the principle. When you would prefer staying in bed rather than getting up a few minutes early to enjoy Christ in the Word, remember the principle. We all need to pray, "Lord, have mercy on me that I would be a part of the firstfruit, and that I would be an overcomer."

In Revelation 22:12 and 20 the Lord Jesus gave us a warning, saying, "Yes, I come quickly." Our loving response should be, "Amen. Come, Lord Jesus!" Our desire should be to love the Lord supremely. We should be sober and watchful for His second coming. By His mercy we may escape the coming hour of trial to meet Him as one of His precious overcomers. Amen. Come, Lord Jesus!

Questions

1. Explain the secret coming and the open coming of Christ. Give references.

2. Who are the firstfruits?

3. What should we do to prepare ourselves for the judgement seat of Christ?

Quoted Portions from (Lee/LSM) Publications

1. *Life Study of Revelation,* pp. 51-61.

2. *Life Study of Romans,* pp. 336-340.

3. *The Kingdom,* pp. 372-374, 385-387, 529-530.

Lesson Twenty-Four

CHRIST IN ETERNITY

Scripture Reading

Rev. 20:11-12, 15; 2 Pet. 3:10; Rev. 21:1-2; John 1:29;
Psa. 46:4; Ezek. 47:5-9; John 7:38; 6:35, 57;
Rev. 2:7; 22:14, 19; 21:9; 22:17

Outline

I. The New Jerusalem in the new heaven and new earth
   A. The redeeming God
   B. The river of water of life
   C. The tree of life
II. The Spirit and the bride

Text

At the end of the millennial kingdom Satan will be thrown into the lake of fire to burn forever. Then, Christ will sit on the great white throne to judge the dead unbelievers of all the ages. In Revelation 20, John wrote, "And I saw a great white throne and Him who sat upon it, from whose face earth and heaven fled away, and no place was found for them. And I saw the dead, the great and the small, standing before the throne, and books were opened; and another book was opened, which is the book of life. And the dead were judged by the things which were written in the books, according to their works.... And if anyone was not found written in the book of life, he was cast into the lake of fire" (vv. 11-12, 15).

After this judgment, the old heaven and the old earth will pass away and eternity will begin with a new heaven and a new earth (2 Pet. 3:10; Rev. 21:1). By then, Christ will have eliminated every negative thing in the universe including Satan, his followers, and the world. Then the purpose of the ages will have been fulfilled. Through Christ's work, man will have been fully redeemed, transformed, glorified, and built up into the corporate expression of the Triune God. What a Christ! What an accomplishment!

I. THE NEW JERUSALEM IN THE NEW HEAVEN AND NEW EARTH

In eternity, Christ will continue to rule, to feed, and to supply His people. Old things will have passed away. The new heaven and new earth will be brought in and the New Jerusalem will descend from God out of heaven. The New Jerusalem is not a physical city; rather it symbolizes what God is to His people and how His people will be fully mingled with Him. In the center of this symbolic city is the throne of God and of the Lamb, out from which flows a river of water of life.

A. The Redeeming God

In the New Jerusalem we will still know Christ as our redeeming God. In Revelation 22:1 we see the throne of God and of the Lamb. There is only one throne since God is in the Lamb and the Lamb is in God. This Lamb is the redeeming God. Because man fell, the creating God became a man (John 1:1, 14), and this man was called the Lamb of God (John 1:29). The creating God became the redeeming God to take away the sins of the world. Praise the Lord that we have been saved by the redeeming God! We were condemned to be in the eternal lake of fire; but instead, for eternity we shall thank the "Lamb-God" that He saved us. We shall have an eternal remembrance of His great redemption. Praise the "Lamb-God!"

B. The River of Water of Life

Do not think that in eternity God merely sits on His throne. Out of the throne proceeds a river of water of life. By this river, God will continue to dispense Himself into us for our eternal enjoyment.

The river, as typified by the rivers in Genesis 2:10-14, Psalm 46:4, and Ezekiel 47:5-9, signifies the abundance of life in its flow. It is one river, flowing through the four directions of the holy city like the four heads of the one river in

Genesis 2:10-14. This one river with its riches becomes many rivers in our experience, as indicated in John 7:38.

The water of life is a symbol of God in Christ as the Spirit flowing Himself into His redeemed people to be their life and life supply. It is typified by the water that came out of the cleft rock (Exo. 17:6; Num. 20:11) and is symbolized by the water that flowed out of the pierced side of the Lord Jesus (John 19:34). Here, this water of life becomes a river, proceeding out of the throne of God and of the Lamb to supply and saturate the entire New Jerusalem. Thus, the city is filled with the divine life to express God in His glory of life.

C. The Tree of Life

Revelation 22:2 says, "And on this side and on that side of the river was the tree of life." The one tree of life growing on the two sides of the river signifies that the tree of life is a vine, spreading and proceeding along the flow of the water of life for God's people to receive and enjoy. It fulfills, for eternity, what God intended from the beginning (Gen. 2:9). The tree of life was closed to man due to his fall (Gen. 3:22-24), but opened to believers by the redemption of Christ (Heb. 10:19-20). Today the enjoyment of Christ as the tree of life is the believers' common portion (John 6:35, 57). In the millennial kingdom the overcoming believers will enjoy Christ as the tree of life as their reward (Rev. 2:7). Eventually, in the new heaven and new earth, for eternity, all God's redeemed will enjoy Christ as the tree of life as their eternal portion (22:14, 19).

The tree of life is Christ as our life supply. First, Christ was the Lamb of God for our redemption (John 1:29), and then the tree of life for our life supply (John 6:35). Christ redeemed us to impart Himself into us as the life supply. He is not only the Lamb of God, but also the tree of life.

II. THE SPIRIT AND THE BRIDE

Revelation 21:9 says, "Come here, I will show you the bride, the wife of the Lamb." Who is this Lamb? This Lamb is Christ, the Lamb-God. He is the Bridegroom of the bride

(John 3:29). But notice that Revelation 22:17 says, "The Spirit and the bride say, Come!" It does not say the *Lamb* and the bride; it says the *Spirit* and the bride. These two verses together prove that Christ, the Lamb, is just the Spirit.

This Spirit is the consummation of the entire Triune God. The Spirit as the Bridegroom is the totality and the consummation of the Triune God. He is qualified to be such a husband to marry the wife, who is the consummation of all the redeemed and regenerated people of God. This is a universal couple with divinity marrying humanity.

Here are two consummations. Divinity has gone through a process—through incarnation, crucifixion, resurrection, and ascension—to become the Spirit, the totality, the consummation, of the Triune God to be the Bridegroom. Humanity also has gone through a process—through redemption, regeneration, and transformation—to become the consummation of God's chosen, redeemed, regenerated, and transformed people to be the bride. The consummation of the Triune God and the consummation of God's chosen, redeemed, regenerated, and transformed people become one in a universal marriage. The processed tripartite man will match the processed Triune God forever for His full expression and satisfaction.

What a destiny we have! Yet, we need not wait to enjoy Christ as the Lamb, the river, and the tree of life. Today, as we are still in the process of transformation, we can enjoy a foretaste of our eternal enjoyment. Christ's process is complete, but ours is not. We are the children of God, being transformed that we may be built up as the Body to express Christ eternally. May we go on each day in the experience and enjoyment of Christ's wonderful Person and work. Amen! Hallelujah!

Questions

1. Fellowship with your companions about the various aspects of the New Jerusalem, such as, the redeeming God, the river of life, the tree of life, etc.

2. Write a ten minute prophesy on how Christ's person and work brings sinners like us into a coinherence with the Triune God to produce the New Jerusalem.

Quoted Portions from (Lee/LSM) Publications

1. *Life-study of Revelation,* pp. 215, 665-668, 740, 742-745, 748-749, 758-759.

2. *Stream Magazine Book Two,* pp. 1534-1535.

3. *The Kernel of the Bible,* pp. 199-201.

4. *The Basic Revelation in the Holy Scriptures,* pp. 110-111.

5. *The Central View of the Divine Dispensation,* p. 97.

6. *The Divine Dispensing of the Divine Trinity,* pp. 42-44.

7. *Life-study of Mark,* p. 595.

BOOKS IN THIS SERIES

Living Stream Ministry

Available at
Christian bookstores, or contact Living Stream Ministry
2431 W. La Palma Ave. • Anaheim, CA 92801
1-800-549-5164 • www.livingstream.com